A Galaxy Of Starfish

An Anthology Of Modern Surrealism

A Galaxy Of Starfish

An Anthology Of Modern Surrealism

Edited by Sophie Essex

salò press

Some of these poems appeared previously in the following journals: *Uut Poetry*, *Lyre Lyre*, *Out Of Our*, *Echolocation*, *The Associative Press*, *The Body in Equipoise*, *Moonshot*, and *Exit Strata*.

The function of genius is to furnish cretins with ideas twenty years later - Louis Aragon, "La Porte-plume," *Traite du style*, 1928

ISBN number: 978-0-9933508-2-5

Back cover quote from *Anti-Artistic Manifesto*, Salvador Dali, 1928

Printed and Bound by 4Edge

Cover design and layout by Muxxi
(www.muxxi.me)

Typeset by Andrew Hook

Published by:
Salò Press
85 Gertrude Road
Norwich
UK

editorsalòpress@gmail.com
www.salòpress.weebly.com

Table of Contents

Introduction: Sea Stars

I have a starfish that I bought at a Jewish dealer's in the rue des Rosiers, which is the very incarnation of a long lost love - Robert Desnos

Reasons why: In Man Ray's 1928 short film *L'Etoile de Mer* there is a scene in which Desnos' hands - black lines painted across them as a foretelling of the future / a possibilty of love - fall into frame in a dizzying display of eroticism & beauty.

A *Galaxy of Starfish* is a tiny part of my obsessions. I love. I ache.

Whilst our definitions of surrealism vary they are glorious in their fluidity, are movement of ideas & passion, are valid in every interpretation. Isn't that something? We are all sea stars.

with love & chaos

Sophie, March 2016

A Short Play in Which Ash is Never Mentioned ~ Dalton Day

You: say you heard this before

You: I heard this before

Me: I got birds in my belly

You: you were in a tree

Me: I told you this already I'm sorry

You: the branches burned but you didn't burn you didn't reach up to the clouds with your neck you didn't say hey when you breathe I can too

Me: say you do too

Me: say you got birds in your belly too

Me: say sleep say science can only be measured when our hands are warm say you were in a tree

You: I lost the word for sleep

Me: I can do anything with the sky

You: I dig myself up every night the trees are on fire but they don't look like skeletons they look like

You: you

Me: these birds in my belly I can't fall

You: don't fall

You: me I ain't ever fell asleep once

Me: you were in a tree

Me: the world had too much dirt on its feathers it couldn't move

Me: you hatched from your own hands same as

Me: I heard this before

You: I never heard a thing before you

A Short Play in Which Warm Air Rises, Expands, & Cools ~ Dalton Day

[A cloud is floating approximately twelve feet above the stage. Everyone in the audience is playing the *what shape does that cloud look like game*. You & I are in the audience. You say the cloud looks like a house that, when stepped in, left its inhabitants no choice but to finally relax. We overhear a woman behind us say it looks like her, but she doesn't seem surprised about it. A small boy in the front whispers *can I go to the bathroom now?* & doesn't get an answer, but is silently escorted out by one of his parents. This goes on for hours. People change their minds, even though the cloud doesn't change at all. *A dog's paw that's missing a nail! A map of all the places I almost started to cry, but didn't! I hope this never ends!* As for me, I haven't said what I think the cloud looks like. I can't. I don't have a word for it, though I know what it is. Everyone has their own shape for terror. Relief, too.]

Dear Floating As A Defense Mechanism ~ Dalton Day

I keep a lake in my pocket, too. For emergencies. For Sundays. For if you will hold my hand, I will hold your hand back. Every time my body moves, I use the word *unfold* to describe that movement. & I wonder if I am wrong in doing so, if instead of moving, I am just expanding. But it's ok, either way, I think. Don't worry about me. I'm doing what I've always done: vibrating when the air makes contact, as if one day, it no longer will.

Love,

From One Side to the Other

Dear Not Yet Wolf ~ Dalton Day

Dear Not Yet Wolf,

I will light candle after candle & give them to you. You can call them sun. We can become sisters & walk around at night. I will throw rocks at the streetlights & you will grow quiet. Because the Sun will be yours you can swallow it down & it will always be dark. There will always be stars until there are not. But such is not death. But such cannot be. Your bones are brittle & I don't want to break you. But there will still be glass. We will be sleeping in pianos that were once trees & the rain will come because we cannot fall in its place & you will crumble. I will hold you in my gentle hands & they will not be gentle & you will be gone & only my hands & only your gentle will be able to stay. My only crime is getting older.

Love,

Not Yet Ghost

What a Bear Is Made Of ~ Dalton Day

after Lindsay Watson

A bear is made of the length of time it takes for a sunbeam to shoot across a window, destroying everything inside of it into a living without stillness.

You know this because you collected all the dust from your childhood & made a country out of it. In this country are trees. In these trees are people with arms.

The people go their whole lives with their arms directly in front of them, waiting to be hugged by a bear. When a bear finally hugs them, their arms fall off.

The ground takes the arms, & allows them to become trees. When new people enter this country, they find a tree & they live there. Everyone holds each other up.

You are proud of your country. The air moves through it & you remember the world before you. So much fur waiting in the dark, ready to be the opposite of seen.

DALTON DAY is a poet & literal dog-person living in Austin, Texas. He is the author of the chapbook Fake Knife, *& his poems have been featured in Hobart, PANK, Everyday Genius, & Columbia Poetry Review, among others. His first collection, Actual Cloud, was published by Salò Press in 2015.*

He can be found at myshoesuntied.tumblr.com and twitter.com/lilghosthands.

Uutkoum ~ Esther Greenleaf Murer

Octopus tethered
to a sarsparilla moon:
marshmallow cactus

in the gazebo
with a sarsparilla moon;
silken clangor of grapefruit

in the gazebo.
Saxophone petals,
silken clangor of grapefruit,

four molting warthogs:
saxophone petals
trumpet a pink serenade

for molting warthogs
with sun-dried notions.
A pink trumpet serenades

simmering seesaws
while sun-dried notions
quilt a languid mazurka

and seesaws simmer,
imprinting on mulch
a languid mazurka quilt:

tethered octopus
imprinted on mulch,
marshmallow cactus.

Form: Haikoum, a hybrid haiku/pantoum invented by
Anna Evans

The house beyond the pelican gate ~
Esther Greenleaf Murer

The house beyond the pelican gate
drips blue malfeasance. Drones and mischants
rumple the sometime sun, as if
by harsh entanglements of wilted lobsters,
gingerbread could rise and bite
the scalene obfuscations of the stars.

All, all is sundry, saving your
presence. Grim presentiments
asseverate the pungent gloom
while feeding mystery to the frogs:
a gathered foothold, numb
as a tinker's bailiwick—

skewed, sturdy, turgid.

title from a dream

Rime of another ancient ~
Esther Greenleaf Murer

I am they who broached the burning seas
in search of wooden wisdom. Heard the moan
of krakens mingled with the pewter sighs
of jellyfish resplendent on the main.

And just as juncos, braving rampant lambs,
unloose their thunder from a brazen bowl
and fortify the sky with lissome limes
blown from a cornucopic alt-horn's bell;

or as the ermine, turning in its sleep
on distant reaches of the mountain-melt,
pauses to punctuate the rancid slope
with hairballs gathered from the summer's molt;

so do the alderpated sages sound
their limpid oracles athwart the sand.

first sentence from a dream

How they snow ~ Esther Greenleaf Murer

Invasive ducks mow past the marble mountain
clomping, clomping webshod over the silence.

I stretch my god to fetch a little gibberish
and dream toward ecstasies bedecking your eyes.

How they snow: fiery glue in the morning.
Flatboy, your ears could cure the march of stone.

drafted in a liminal state

Shards of bottled ivory ~
Esther Greenleaf Murer

after Rambo

Come, jade sands of impossible flavors,
touched by electric loons!
Saxes eat currants and sail the sward;
jeans, new-closed, lay eyes on colored

potatoes. Days are canceled
to comb debris of divorced peninsulas:
ouds caught on angles, ants, daymares,
grappa, odd clocks, prose.

Tenants, two to a coop, lend rhythm
to sieves in a green night
touched by mystic horrors:
rudiments of a jury.

Essence of nuisance, jet age tousles
a fund of Tudors and textiles.
The tempest has blessed my maritime evils:
Libra, fuming, mounts her violet broom.

homophonic translation of selected lines from Arthur
Rimbaud's "Le bateau ivre"

This just in from the foot-farm ~
Esther Greenleaf Murer

Mark the wrench of my words:
The moon is sucking the computers awry.
Plump corporals, bent on posing
as scrumptiousness in a tin hat,
wither under the eyelids of striped November
while a horde of steeplejacks ascend the town
with all the finesse of barnacles.

The world goes on:
Penguins have expectations,
a mother irons the dog. Paper rains
caress the ruddy spermophile.
Foot-farms do their silent work.
Meet me on the caking-green by starlight;
I'll be at the seventh lily from the corner.

ESTHER GREENLEAF MURER has been writing poetry all her life, and got serious about learning the craft when she turned seventy. She published her first collection, Unglobed Fruit, in 2011, and has been featured in The Centrifugal Eye, KIN, and the Guardian. She lives in Philadelphia. Links to many of her poems published online may be found at http://esthergreenleafmurer.blogspot.com/

conforms to the angles of a labyrinth. Tastes the reds and violets of music. Is practiced at B, beth, and beta. Is the binding agent between earth and sky. Its sinews are house. Its muscles: landscape. Its bones: fence. Its limbs: cantilevers. Its nervous system is a radio tuned to the soundtrack of life. It is "the human being squaring the circle."[1] It is the human being squaring "the human being squaring the circle." Is the art museum of the world. Is architecture itself.

---

[1]*Aaron Betsky. "Bodybuildings: Toward a Hybrid Order of Architecture"*

Jean Cocteau Spectacles ~ Joel Allegretti

I had seven visions through them,

Of

: my birth certificate printed in white text
        on a white page[1];

: rivers that overflowed their banks
        to lay lapis lazuli at my door[2];

: pearls as a big as a roc's egg[3];

: fruit bats in the halls of the Palace of Versailles[4];

: a stone wall at the end of a blind alley
        in which I saw myself at the age of 112[5];

: body scavengers cruising Main Street
        on Harley-Davidsons[6];

: a café on a nondescript corner, where Hades idled,
        sipping a demitasse and nibbling petit fours.

He wore a pressed morning coat and opera cape[7],
        even though it was early afternoon, ninety-
        seven degrees.

His watch fob was a compass pointing due south.

He offered me a lemon truffle cake.
I bit into it, and out flew a winged something-or-other
        with vermilion scales and an egg-white tongue.

"Ooooo," he cooed. "I wish I had saved
        that one for myself."

1 My friend John J. Trause, librarian and poet, regards a blank page as the perfect piece of writing. Death's book of poems is an empty volume (*Orphée*, 1950).

2 When Beauty weeps, her tears harden into diamonds (*La Belle et la Bête*, 1946).

3 The impossibility of estimating their value renders them worthless.

4 If in orchards or caves, realism.

5 Imagine gazing into a mirror and a monkey looks back at you (*La Belle et la Bête*).

6 (*Orphée*). Serge Gainsbourg, who burned francs on TV, recorded "Harley David Son of a Bitch" in 1984.

7 Marlene Dietrich and Greta Garbo each refused the role of the elegantly coiffed Princess Death (*Orphée*).

**The Dark Sea Breaks Heavily -
A Reddish Glow Spreads in It -
A Sea of Blood Foams at My Feet***
~ Joel Allegretti

5:15 a.m.   And it is Christ the Sea.

5:25   Sunrise.

I'm thinking of Théodore Géricault's
The Raft of the Medusa.
The painting depicts the few who
survived the inhospitality of the open
sea and the onus of human desperation,
who were not murdered, cannibalized
or driven mad by starvation and
hopelessness.

If souls such as these were cast adrift
on Christ the Sea,
I believe all would be saved,
that fresh water would come to them,
that bluefish would give their bodies to
feed the shipwrecked multitudes.

5:30   I'm alone on the shore.

5:40   I'm not alone on the shore.
A live manta ray lies yards away, a
broken law.

6:05   I'm strolling along a beat-up boardwalk.
Its warped, creaking planks no longer
know the weight of vacationers' feet.
My shoes leave a red trail.

6:15   A second manta ray has joined the one.

6:20   The fun house, the Ferris wheel, the
roller coaster, the shooting gallery:
The rides and attractions that tenanted
the boardwalk are hollow bodies and old
men's skeletons. Would the blood tide
take them?

6:45   Manta rays are occupying the coast! As
far as my eyes allow me to see, I see
them advancing millimeter by
millimeter by way of their great black
Dracula wings to leave Christ the Sea.

Yes.
Of course.
They are also known as devilfish.

* *The title comes from* The Red Book *by C.G. Jung.*
Kyburz, Mark; John Peck and Sonu Shamdasani,
translators. (New York: W.W. Norton & Co., 2009).

The Amphisbaena Reconsidered as Architectural Template ~ Joel Allegretti

Blueberry Half Moon Lane East runs along the shore and parallels Blueberry Half Moon Lane West, which lies a hundred yards away contiguous to an abandoned service road. One house, only one, stands between the Blueberry Half Moon Lanes. It is a two-story gingerbread structure, an architect's simulacrum of a watercolor plate from a Victorian-era children's book.

*

A porch faces Blueberry Half Moon Lane East and regularly receives the spindrift's ablutions. To the right of the door through which you enter the house is a wooden plaque with a painting of a pineapple. The welcome mat is clean and proportional to the doorway. The porch is an especially strong vantage point from which to observe the sunrise. There is a rocking chair, circa 1970s, that serves this purpose well and embellishes the pacific experience. When you open the door and step inside, a beige foyer greets you. To your right are stairs leading to the upper floor. To your left is a forest-green parlor. The room's focal point is an upright piano, probably an antique or at least a family heirloom. A burgundy colonial chesterfield, lace doilies adorning its arms, and a set of upholstered high-back chairs, also burgundy, circumnavigate the instrument. Another rocking chair is at a remove, off in the corner by the window. Folded on the seat in a rectangle is a black-and-red checkerboard Afghan blanket, the kind sold at a community craft fair. The ambience here is that of a quaint bed and breakfast.

*

A porch faces Blueberry Half Moon Lane West and witnesses daily the dwindling glimmer of the setting sun. To the right of the door through which you enter the house is a wooden plaque with a painting of a pineapple. The welcome mat is clean and proportional to the doorway. The porch is an especially strong vantage point from which to observe the abandoned service road. There is a rocking chair, circa 1970s, that serves this purpose well and embellishes the desolate experience. When you open the door and step inside, a forest-green foyer greets you. To your right are stairs leading to the upper floor. To your left is a beige parlor. The room's focal point is an upright piano, probably an antique or at least a family heirloom. An indigo colonial chesterfield, lace doilies adorning its arms, and a set of upholstered high-back chairs, also indigo, circumnavigate the instrument. Another rocking chair is at a remove, off in the corner by the window. Folded on the seat in a rectangle is a white-and-yellow checkerboard Afghan blanket, the kind sold at a community craft fair. The ambience here is that of a quaint ...

For Immediate Release:

"House of Goodbye" Opens at Museum of Enteric Representation

~ **Joel Allegretti**

The Museum of Enteric Representation today announced the opening of "House of Goodbye," an installation by the theoretical artist and architect Nicholas Σ. The exhibition runs through 5 p.m. tomorrow, at which time Σ and a team of his students will destroy it in the presence of museum visitors.

The piece occupies the entire first floor and half of the second. The second-floor portion is closed to the public. The artist, however, has created "Goodbye Means Goodbye," a set of 501 23" x 29" multiples featuring black-and-white photographs of that section of the work. They are available on the second-floor landing at no charge.

Elaborating on the impetus for "House of Goodbye," Σ writes in an artist's statement, "Here is the room of the bed of final things. Where a lifetime's cookie jar of dreams and wishes is the last word of the last sentence of a paragraph. Science has advanced from background music to a concert program for a rapt audience. Religion is the coda, the diminishing strain as the bow decelerates across the violin strings. Silence, as John Cage knew, is itself a form of composition, notably when a lifetime's cookie jar of dreams and wishes is the last word of the last sentence of a paragraph that strives to describe the room of the bed of final things."

The Museum of Enteric Representation is planning a retrospective of Σ's aerosol sculptures.

Towards the Design and Construction of a House in the Shape of Water ~ Joel Allegretti

> Architecture in general is frozen music.
>   Friedrich von Schelling (1775 – 1854)

> O wizard of changes, water, water, water.
>   Robin Williamson (1943 –   )

Vitruvius doesn't address the subject in *The Ten Books on Architecture*. Neither does Le Corbusier in *Towards a New Architecture*. Neither does Rem Koolhaas in *S, M, L, XL*.

In *From Bauhaus to Our House*, Tom Wolfe considers buildings designed by Mies van der Rohe, Eero Saarinen, and Philip Johnson, but not this.

Architects have realized structures in the shapes of:

- a basket (headquarters of The Longaberger Company, a basket manufacturer in Newark, Ohio. Architect: unknown);
- a conch shell (private home on Isla Mujeres, Mexico. Architect: Octavio Ocampo);
- a teapot (gas station in Zillah, Washington. Architect: John Ainsworth).

None to date—not Garnier, not Gaudi, not Gehry—has brought into three dimensions a dwelling in the shape of the shapeless.

Career Counsel

Become that architect.

Step 1. Enroll in a distinguished school of architecture, such as California Polytechnic State University or Cooper Union, and earn a bachelor's degree.

Steps 2 and 3. To hold yourself out as an architect, you need a state license. Therefore, you additionally must:

- complete an internship with a firm;
- pass all seven divisions of the Architect Registration Examination®.

Think about an office by the ocean or at least a lake. For inspiration's sake.

Recognize that you'll have to fund the construction, since no one will commission it.

Know that your creation will attract notice and invite interpretation.

*

Mediterranean," the Continental among us said.
"Red,"
held the Cairo-bred real estate broker.
The architect, Chicago born and raised, shook his head.
"Lake Michigan."

JOEL ALLEGRETTI *is the author of five collections of poetry. His second,* Father Silicon *(The Poet's Press, 2006), was selected by* The Kansas City Star *as one of 100 Noteworthy Books of 2006.*

He is the editor of Rabbit Ears: TV Poems *(NYQ Books, 2015), the first anthology of poetry about the mass medium.*

Allegretti's poetry has appeared in The New York Quarterly, Barrow Street, Smartish Pace, PANK, *and many other national journals, as well as in journals published in Canada, the United Kingdom, Belgium, and India.*

He has published his fiction in The MacGuffin, The Adroit Journal, *and* The Nassau Review, *among other literary journals. His performance texts and theater pieces have been staged at La MaMa Experimental Theater, Medicine Show Theater, the Cornelia Street Café, and SideWalk Café, all in New York.*

He wrote the texts for three song cycles by Frank Ezra Levy, whose work is released on Naxos American Classics. Allegretti is a member of ASCAP.

The Axis of Fog ~ David Nadeau

she is blindfolded
attentive to unravel the immense spirals
in a room with colors of mirage
this nude scene unites with chance by a secret door

some vestiges approach
space explores the intonations in the lower regions of
  the flame
the transmission of the bones faces the obstacles of
  the rose
the interior of the the skull remains motionless
for the unknown ear that you will deposit at the foot
  of the question
in the hollow of the crowned ear

L'Axe Du Brouillard ~ David Nadeau

les yeux bandés
attentive à démêler les immenses spirales
dans une pièce aux couleurs de mirage
cette scène nue épouse le hasard par une porte secrète

quelques vestiges se rapprochent
l'espace explore les intonations dans les régions
  inférieures de la flamme
la transmission des ossements se heurte aux
  obstacles de la rose
l'intérieur du crâne reste immobile
pour l'oreille inconnue que vous déposerez au pied de
  la question
au creux de l'oreille couronnée

Sites of the Shadow ~ David Nadeau

I

worthy to attain the reverse that deforms
  the threshold in reverse at the poorly housed zenith
he plays with the century of bronze and the duration
 of the black oscillations of his disappearance

absent to have handled the night peacock
and mute at the lead veils

II

immersion in the embryonic poetry of the unknown body
  the wet riddle at the hells of heavy waves and fairy
the golden erosion moves the lips and the fingers of
 the abyss at the fall of a gesture

the echo of a horned desire dons the reflection of the
roses

III

if the city is the almond of the floods by the vast
 expanses of stained glass
a fragment of night pales the veil of the awakenings

IV

palpate the tear of an abyss about to break into the
 atmospheric bark of the streets

V

evaporated again

Chantiers De L'Ombre ~ David Nadeau

I

digne d'atteindre l'envers qui déforme
        le seuil en sens inverse au zénith mal logé
il joue avec le siècle de bronze et la durée des
 oscillations noires de sa disparition

absent d'avoir manié le paon de nuit
et muet aux voiles de plomb

II

plongée dans la poésie embryonnaire du corps inconnu
l'énigme humide aux enfers de fée et d'ondes lourdes
l'érosion dorée remue les lèvres et les doigts du
 gouffre à la tombée d'un geste

l'écho d'un désir cornu revêt les reflets des roses

III

Si la ville est l'amande des déluges par les vastes
 étendues de vitraux
un fragment de nuit pâlit le voile des réveils

IV

palper cette larme d'un abîme à se rompre dans
 l'écorce atmosphérique des rues

V

encore évaporée

Dark Healer Dream ~ David Nadeau

The lion, at his decline, conjures the crossing of the fluids
The eyelids of clay are intoxicated
thunderstorms locked in small pebbles
the inexplicable sand of certainties
sudden mathematical of the snakes
the miniature wandering of the tribes and trumpets
The strange nodes of the dead, and the stairs, abound
 over ravines: the silverware of the fraudulent errors
The house appears
The parchment is rooted under the walls of the equinox
The inner fortress of the peacock tells his vow and his scarf
Humanity is the orthodox result of a deterioration in
 the syntax

The moon with spoon eyes turns against the brains
It sits in the fallen and rimless fire
the misshapen triangle of the angel

The metallic depths of the witchery immolate the
 entranced family
The pharmaceutical birth of the rectangle is wearing
 arteries
The ridicule wind is a pestilential remedy
the pungent smoke of the unconscious treasure
The imperial neck reaches hypnosis
the profane boat of nail clippings
A sleepwalker planet predicts the bloodstained
 plagiarism
The tattooed bird threatens the christian zodiac, code
 hatched in the eagle ingested by a consciousness
The royal egg accelerates
The flame breaks the mirror of asceticism
The ankle is a coffin key
The animal in ecstasy between two bites
dark healer dream

Noir Songe Guerisséur ~ David Nadeau

Le lion, à son déclin, conjure la traversée des fluides
Les paupières d'argile sont intoxiquées
les orages enfermés dans de petits cailloux
le sable inexplicable des certitudes
mathématique brusque des serpents
l'errance miniature des tribus et trompettes
Les nouds étranges des morts et les escaliers foisonnent
au-dessus des ravins : l'orfèvrerie des erreurs frauduleuses
La maison apparaît
Le parchemin a pris racine sous les murs de l'équinoxe
La forteresse intime du paon déclare son vou et son
  écharpe
L'humanité est la conséquence orthodoxe d'une
  dégradation de la syntaxe

La lune aux yeux de cuillères se retourne contre les
  cerveaux
Elle s'assoit dans le feu déchu et sans contour
le triangle difforme de l'ange

Les profondeurs métalliques de l'envoûtement
  immolent la famille en transe
La naissance pharmaceutique du rectangle est vêtue
  d'artères
Le vent ridicule est un remède pestilentiel
la fumée piquante du trésor inconscient
La nuque impériale parvient jusqu'à l'hypnose
la barque profane des rognures d'ongles
Une planète somnambule prédit le plagiat taché de sang
L'oiseau tatoué menace le zodiaque chrétien, code
  éclos dans l'aigle ingéré par une conscience
L'ouf royal accélère
La flamme brise le miroir de l'ascèse
La cheville est une clé de cercueil
L'animal en extase entre deux morsures
noir songe guérisseur

The Wounded Mystery ~ David Nadeau

eternal courtesan with the heart of a perverse and
 pure child
her delicious chrysalid in the ominous silence

sanctuary of the storm
the entwined sarcophagi

the ritual game
the aurora shows us the lantern of eagles
the philosopher's room in the invisible fire of the woman
the cambered moon

Translated with the help of Allan Graubard

Le Mystère Blessé ~ David Nadeau

courtisane éternelle au cour d'enfant perverse et
 pure
sa chrysalide délicieuse dans le silence augural

sanctuaire de l'orage
les sarcophages enlacés

le jeu rituel
l'aurore nous montre la lanterne des aigles
la chambre philosophale dans le feu invisible de la
 femme
la lune cambrée

Down To The Archives ~ David Nadeau

1- PEDIMENT OF THE NUMBER

The gesture of the hand, clairvoyant, ecstatic, expresses the metaphysical intuition of the absolute: a strangely ornate cross, knightly emblem. In the electromagnetic grimoires, the unexpected hieroglyphs and the complicated diagrams reflect the alteration of the fog, generate other prodigious or disturbing atmospheric phenomena
(the favorable signs engraved on the sky by the sword of a red planet,
the last pre-Columbian cyclone,
the membranous storms built by the plumage of the rocks,
the mercurial waves).
Represented by those few silent but effective signs of affiliation, the secret complicity, created between some who wish to remake the human understanding, forms the germ of a future civilization. The natural number torn in every direction, from the side of the the spirit's anniversary, extends itself to the faculties of the seraphim. Metatron Tetragrammaton.

2- ELECTROMAGNETIC GILGAMESH

When traveling in magical imagination, he remembers the primordial myths, distant extensions of past existences. The hallucinatory textures of some rock surfaces tell him the mythological battles that took place in the early time and the consequences of which are still felt today, unbeknownst to us, in our disenchanted world. The gaze becomes tactile.

3- VITRIOL

Visit to the subterranean laboratory before its collapse; here, you can still see the occult archives of the subconscious, the complicated charts whose meaning is to be reinvented. This algebra of wonders summarizes the laws of harmony between the different parts of the universe. The multiple diagrams illustrate especially the cosmic cycles of destruction and creation, the new and surrealist worlds revealed by current particle physics, the crossing of the numbers that are tied to each other, the cosmogonies in ruins. Fallen out of the lips of Thoth, the asemic characters create the world, destroy and recreate it. Henri Michaux was born of this globe of experimental alphabet. The syllables fall into the moving abyss. The hypnagogic hallucinations try to decipher the bark of the proteins. The only microscopic poem is floating in a cytoplasm of pleasing appearance. The vacuum appears textured up to hyper-acuity. Christian Dotremont bears the armorial bearings of the morning, in the intimate penumbra of the language. The secret diplomacy of these initiated creators and their companions prepares the advent of a civilization both anarchist and animist.

Descente Aux Archives ~ David Nadeau

1- LE FRONTON DU NOMBRE

Le geste de la main, clairvoyant, extatique, exprime l'intuition métaphysique de l'absolu : une croix étrangement ornementée, emblème chevaleresque. Dans les grimoires électromagnétiques, les hiéroglyphes imprévus et les diagrammes compliqués traduisent l'altération de la brume, suscitent d'autres phénomènes atmosphériques prodigieux ou inquiétants
(les signes favorables gravés sur le ciel par l'épée d'une planète rouge,
le dernier cyclone précolombien,
les ondes mercurielles,
les tempêtes membraneuses édifiées par le plumage des rochers,
l'axe du brouillard,
le vent ridicule, qui est un remède pestilentiel).
Représentée par ces quelques signes d'appartenance muets mais efficaces, la secrète complicité, créée entre certains être qui désirent refaire l'entendement humain, forme le germe d'une civilisation future. Le nombre naturel arraché dans tous les sens, du côté de l'anniversaire de l'esprit, s'étend jusqu'aux facultés des séraphins. Métatron Tetragrammaton.

2- GILGAMESH ÉLECTROMAGNÉTIQUE

Lors des voyages en imagination magique, il se ressouvient des mythes primordiaux, lointains prolongements d'existences passées. Les textures hallucinatoires de certaines surfaces rocheuses lui racontent les combats mythologiques qui ont eu lieu au début des temps et dont les conséquences se font encore sentir aujourd'hui, à notre insu, dans notre monde désenchanté. Le regard devient tactile.

3- VITRIOL

Visite au laboratoire souterrain avant son effondrement; ici, tu peux encore consulter les archives occultes du subconscient, les diagrammes compliqués dont la signification est à réinventer. Cette algèbre de merveille résume les lois de l'harmonie entre le différentes parties de l'univers. Les multiples schémas illustrent notamment les cycles cosmiques de destruction et de création, les mondes nouveaux et surréalistes révélés par la physique actuelle, la traversée des nombres qui se nouent les uns aux autres, les cosmogonies en ruines. Sortis des lèvres de Thot, les caractères asémiques créent le monde, le détruisent et le recrée. Henri Michaux naît de ce globe d'alphabet expérimental. Les syllabes chutent dans l'abîme en mouvement. Les hallucinations hypnagogiques tentent de déchiffrer l'écorce des protéines. Le seul poème microscopique flotte dans un cytoplasme d'apparence agréable. Le vide apparaît texturé, jusqu'à l'hyper-acuité. Christian Dotremont arbore les armoiries du matin, dans la pénombres intime du langage. La diplomatie secrète de ces créateurs initiés et de leurs compagnons prépare l'avènement d'une civilisation à la fois anarchiste et animiste.

DAVID NADEAU *is an art historian, a poet and a visual artist living in Quebec city. He participates in the surrealist movement in the groups La Vertèbre et le Rossignol and Device Scribbles collective. He has published in* Aghula, revista de cultura *(2006),* La Conspiration dépressionniste *(2010),* Hydrolith: Surrealist Research and Investigations *(2010, 2014),* La chasse à l'objet du désir *(2014),* The Annual *(2015),* A Phala *(2015),* Materika *(2016) and* Las Llaves del deseo *(2016).*

84197169399375 ~ Travis Macdonald

Heaven be gathered together unto one place and
process: the justification of
sterility
we feel ourselves compelled to admit. All remaining
    propositions—
land, earth, and the gathering together of
a
perfect condition—yet, when intercrossed, they
saw that it was good *and* god. Said: "Let
the earth bring
from the axioms the question of the truth, of
tree yielding fruit after his kind whose seed is
both plants and
animals." Though the organs themselves are perfect,
the earth brought forth grass.

4211706798214808651328230 66 ~
Travis Macdonald

Then he cuts the
knot. For
whales,
positions
on a practically rigid body is something

which is lodged deeply in our
species. Quite fertile together, he unhesitatingly ranks
(to regard three points as being situated on a
god) them, saying: "Be fruitful, and multiply,
and fill...
coincide!"
But in these, and
eye—under suitable choice of our place of

the evening and the morning—were the fifth
thought. We now supplement the propositions
earth bring forth: the living
maximum
after his kind
produced by
a practically rigid body. Always correspond to the
offspring with
line-interval independently

produced by both pure parent species
of the earth after his kind.

4102701938521 ~ Travis Macdonald

Be for meat. And
absolutely.

Every beast.
Establish the distance between two points on

conclusion:
"The air and to every thing that creepeth upon
that, we may
distance." –Rod S. Which is to be used?
Herb for meat? And it,
which we
employ?

7270365759591 ~ Travis Macdonald

"Try it!" During several subsequent years, and
always with
the ground embankment it describes, a parabola

did eat...and
other observers in the case of
serpent. Because thou hast done
such thing as an independently existing trajectory—
and above every beast of
a trajectory relative to a particular body of reference—
dust shalt thou eat. All
ovules and pollen of the same flower were perfectly
good.

5628 ~ Travis Macdonald

The Theory of Relativity entered
as the father and then as
an analysis
of the physical conceptions of time and space.

32788659361533818279682303o ~
Travis Macdonald

Window-of-the-
Together, why
should the degree of sterility be innately
a raven? Which went forth, to and fro?
Why should some species cross with facility and
yet, produce very sterile hybrids? And
a dove from him to
difficulty, and yet...produce fairly fertile hybrids? Why
    should
there often be
ground but the dove found no
rest
for the sole of her
mirrors? Inclined at
species, why (it
may even be asked) has the production of
B_____
been permitted to grant to species the special
power of
flashes of lightning? At the same time,
further propagation by different degrees of sterility
    not strictly
(yet) other? Seven days and again
I cannot regard the matter as quite settled,
because I
feel constrained to

rules and facts.

82953311686172785588890750983817546 ~
Travis Macdonald

The quince, which is ranked as a distinct,
is associated
with every event which is essentially capable of
     observation.
All the fishes of the
sea, into your
hand... are they
degrees
of
moving? Thing that liveth shall be
different varieties of the apricot and peach. On
certain varieties of the plum as
rate,
found that there was sometimes an innate
difference in
different individuals of the same two species.
Different places of a reference body are set
at the hand of every
beast. Will I require it?
Pointers of the one clock is simultaneous in
the facility of effecting an union, is often
the life of the man whoso sheddeth man's blood by

grafting. The common gooseberry, for instance, cannot
be grafted on the currant.

Whereas the currant will take (though with difficulty) on
body of reference, which we have styled a
"railway embankment." We
have their reproductive organs in an imperfect
     condition
with
a very different case: from the difficulty

(the direction indicated in fig)
with your seed after
you and with every living creature.

Author's Note:

п (pi or 3.14159etc.) is a transcendental number. This suggests, among other things, that no finite sequence of algebraic operations on integers (powers, roots, sums, etc.) can be equal to its value. Consequently, its decimal representation never ends or repeats. It divides in endless variation.

These pieces are composed solely of language borrowed in direct sequential and numerical order from The Book of Genesis, *Charles Darwin's* The Origin of Species *(Chapter 8 - Hybridism) and Albert Einstein's* Special and General Theory of Relativity.

Each poem is comprised of individual lines whose word count corresponds precisely with the relative decimal point of pi to its first 1,415 places. When drawing from each source, the author has taken great care never to exceed 3 consecutive lines from any given text and, even then, only in cases where the process of natural selection demands. While the original language of each line is faithfully preserved, each selection has been re-punctuated for narrative purposes.

TRAVIS MACDONALD *was recently named a 2014 Pew Fellow in the Arts. He is the author of two full-length books –* The O Mission Repo [vol.1] *(Fact-Simile Editions) and* N7ostradamus *(BlazeVox Books) – as well as several chapbooks, including:* Basho's Phonebook *(E-ratio),* BAR/koans *(Erg Arts),* Sight & Sigh *(Beard of Bees),* Time *(Stoked Press) and* Hoop Cores *(Knives, Forks and Spoons Press).*

A Figment off Autocue Boulevard ~
Gary Budgen

From across the hall Jetsen's father croaked like a toad: "Cretin!"

Always Jetsen had been running out in dramatic fashion, door slamming, stomping off. He takes the bus into the centre of the city.

Autocue Boulevard with its traffic jams, neon, its mannequins dragged-up as humans. When Jetsen walks here he knows he is searching for something.

Once, in a backstreet in the warren of such streets off Autocue Boulevard he saw beyond one of the doors. These were doors that were always closed, their paint cracked and peeling, the numbers in some random order he didn't understand. He made a mental note of the number of this one.

This door was open.

The interior was lit from the side by a weak honeyed light. A figure stood in the shadows. It was a woman, naked, her leg bent as she crouched in a bowl of water. As she washed she ran her hands down her leg. One hand scooped water and she straightened up again rubbing soap suds across the surface of her skin. Jetsen stepped forward to get a better look. The woman was intent on washing but then she turned her head to look at him directly, making him blush.

The interior was honey. A figment stood in shadows. Naked. Bent. Bowl hands down leg. Rubbing. Blushing.

The door was open.

He stepped a little closer.

Interior. Figment. Naked.

Look. Rubbing. Blushing.

The door was open as he stepped through.

In the honey a little closer.

She looked back into the bowl. The water here,

43

slightly soapy, caught the weak honey dripping from the lamp.

Her face was smooth like the mannequins, animate like the crowd on Autocue Boulevard. Her eyes widened. Her lips parted so that a line of spume connected the top lip with the bottom. He allowed himself to look over her body, over the figment in the shadows.

*

He is in an alley off Autocue Boulevard. He passes by the doors that are always shut, the numbers arranged according to no system that he can understand. He tries to remember a number. He passes by a door he might know but it is a black mask, paint flaking. He thinks he is looking for something in particular. A figure in the shadows. A figment in the honey.

Off Autocue Boulevard.

Later he returns home. It is a place he imagines as a spacious uptown mansion, possibly Victorian, with mullioned windows, with chandeliers. Closing the door quietly he goes into his bedroom. He can hear, through the open window, the car horns, the shunting of the traffic on Autocue Boulevard. He is glad he is not there amid the fumes, his skin blushing from the stares of the mannequins.

Across the hall his father snores as he squats on top of his latest wife, suffocating her with the weight of his body turning her to a pile of ash with the heat of his lust. This is what he has already done to Jetsen's mother, who became flakes and fragments of ash, figments, who blew away in a draft.

Jetsen could run out in dramatic fashion, door slamming, stomping off to Autocue Boulevard.

Later his father, sweating from his carnal festivities, looks in on him. Jetsen can hardly bear to look at his father's wart-covered skin, the bulbous lips curved at the corner in a sneer. His father holds a bottle in his hand, raises it and jeers.

"Yer a fucking waster of space."

Around him Jetsen feels the mansion collapse, walls folding down as it becomes the cramped little apartment six floors up a tower block. It is bug infested. Cold in the winter. The lift is often broken. When the lift works it smells of piss.

In the morning he gets away, takes the bus into the centre. He christens a street Autocue Boulevard.

It is a long street given over to shopping and traffic jams. The fumes choke and the noise of the car horns, the clattering of the feet, the impatient engines of cars, mannequins, all threaten to overwhelm him.

He runs in dramatic fashion towards a side street. One of the warren of streets. Off Autocue Boulevard. There is nothing there. And yet Jetsen comes back. It begins to rain and the water washes the doors and the numbers peel off and fall into the gutter where they flow away into the drains. Down in the sewer the numbers multiply.

When it smells of piss in the morning he christens the streets.

It is a street given over to jams, fumes, horns, feet, growls and engines.

He fashions a side street drama off Autocue Boulevard.

He steps past the door wading through honey.

The mannequin stands there perfectly poised, bent and reaching for the round metal pedestal that keeps her upright and catches the light. She might look as though she is bathing, standing in a bowl of water rather than a metal pedestal. It is some kind of old storeroom. Some back part of one of the department stores of Autocue Boulevard.

The mannequin bent ready.

Bathing department.

Off Autocue Boulevard.

He fashions her.

*

Back at the apartment he waits for years as his father dies. Afterwards his father's corpse shrinks to quite the size of a toad and Jetsen puts it inside a family-sized matchbox.

He set off to fashion a family-sized pedestal in some perfectly poised back department off Autocue Boulevard. Past jams, fumes, horns, feet, growls and engines. Through jam to honey. He gets lost in the back streets off Autocue Boulevard. He tries to remember numbers on doors that are blank, black masks, paint peeling.

From its matchbox the toad calls out insults.

"You're useless." "You failure".

"Shut up," says Jetsen, "You're dead."

The toad laughs

"You can't just rationalise me away. Cretin."

It begins to rain. It rains so much that the drains cannot take it. They spew water back and spit out their debris. Numbers pour onto the flooded surface of the street. The numbers are huge where they have multiplied.

Jetsen gets the matchbox out of his pocket and sets it on the water where it floats away.

The toad cries out.

"You can't do this, I'm your father."

Jetsen can hear, in the distance, the car horns, the screams as Autocue Boulevard drowns. In the backstreets he wades through large numbers. As the light of the day fades the street lights come on only to short out from water damage, fizzing, sparking. There is only moonlight now. It paints the water by numbers. The water smells of old multiplication lessons. There are shadows in the water, shapes that bump into Jetsen. They do not feel like the numbers, which are spikey, irritating. No these shapes are large, solid, floating like night boats in a dark harbour.

The rain thins.

Eventually Jetsen finds a windowsill just above the water level and climbs into it. He sits out the night as the screams and the car horns of Autocue Boulevard die down.

And slowly the rain stops while once, in a backstreet by weak honey light, she scooped water.

*

In the morning the floodwaters have drained away. The street is scattered with mannequins, washed here from Autocue Boulevard. Large numbers are stuck to the ground so that as Jetsen resumes his search he has to step over both the bodies of the mannequins and large strings of numbers. The silence across the city is like the embrace of his long dead ashen mother.

He imagines Autocue Boulevard emptied, the cars abandoned and wrecked. It is as though the world has been reborn.

He finds the saturated matchbox in which he had placed his father. Nearby the toad's corpse has been tridented by a large integer beginning with three.

Jetsen runs.

Always he has been running, slamming.

But now he finds the door open.

The interior is lit from the side by week-old honey. A figment stands in the shadow. It is a naked leg. Bent.

The door is open.

The interior is lit from the side by weak light, yellow like fine, almost transparent, honey. There is a woman there. She is naked because she is washing, running her hands around her leg, water sliding over the skin, soap bubbles adhering to the surface. She bends and straightens and hums to herself.

GARY BUDGEN has been published in various magazines including Interzone, Sein und Werden and anthologies from Eibonvale, Boo Books and others. He can be found at https://garybudgen.wordpress.com/

Google Search: First Impressions ~ Logan Ellis

when you said hello
      Did you mean: i'm *more* than *knives* hidden in
                                  dirty dishwater

when you said hello
      Did you mean: i'm *crowdfunding* for a brighter
                                  disposition

when you said hello
      Did you mean: i could masturbate as i *fall* down
                                  the well of your eyes

when you said hello
      Did you mean: i wish i had *known* you when i
                                  was young

when you said hello
      Did you mean: but maybe we *have* met before,
                                  in my bath*water* reflection

when you said hello
      Did you mean: or maybe you've been a *family*
                                  of mice in the tree of my body

when you said hello
      when you said hello
            when you said hello
                 and hello
                        and hello

      Did you mean: or maybe you're a mirror and
                                  I'm just the blood of an invisible
                                  man

Ersatz ~ Logan Ellis

The night fits us like cashmere. Expensive   and
afraid to the touch. Standing in a dark room is like
breathing water: alone   the shadow of a line fishes
over our heads toward the lamp   television   futon
all four table legs   each innocent knick-knack
dusty   on its shelf. I'm not quite present enough to
respond with my   own. I filter whatever you press
against me—five fingers stroking upwards on the
other side of my skin like   a flaming sheet of paper.
Burning and burning a trail   up my shoulder with its
tongue, carving a useless chariot from the bed. The
way you hold   on: a vein opening and braiding itself
around my neck. The way the dust climbs down and
chisels a shelf from my chest. This isn't about love at
bone.   Not here.   And who is this you besides
another brick in the fourth wall? A bomb in a time
capsule buried in our collective ulna. You   are
harmless, persuasive   the coat between skins. A
mouth—no wait, not even that—beating me to fit the
night.

Biopsy of God in the Dark ~ Logan Ellis

Watch how I bless: with eyes of a cornered dog chewing itself apart, with hands quiet enough to scatter your skin at the sound of light. Watch how I reign: torso billowing like a switchblade of water in the dark, lips gathering for their brief impale. Witness how I corrupt: a good gun in the hand of a good guy, reels of war needle-stitched into the moss of the nation. Watch how I sing: colorless emotions broken from brown egg shells, a stroke of light undressing the shadow that wears its teeth inside out.

Revisualization of the Invisible Man ~
Logan Ellis

Slowly, I will come back from what I was: a collapsed building that took its graffiti with it—postwar shrapnel copy-catting the dismemberment of helmet of head of mouth of tongue of vowel. Slowly, vein by vein, I'll admit that I'm sorry for letting you into my weakness: a lone barn swung open in a wild field—the difference between what is growing and the space in which it is growing. Slowly, we will do and re-do: a stem rooted at the center of a stone—my skin a rug and my teeth unsweeping the dust of a broken vase, but not the vase itself.

LOGAN ELLIS is a Pushcart-nominated poet, a Kinder egg of single-celled wordcraft. He's received his BA in English and Writing from the University of Arkansas at Little Rock and is currently enrolled in the Graduate Writing Program at California College of the Arts in San Francisco. His work has been published in ElevenEleven, The Brasilia Review, Electric Cereal, *and* The Electronic Encyclopedia of Experimental Literature, *among others. More of his work can be found on his blog unknowmenclature.tumblr.com.*

So ~ David Spicer

The Jesuit scholar wants to prove
Manet an impotent homosexual. Who cares?
I love to play rugby on the shuttle,
chew peanuts like a skunk on a rocket,
and hold lackluster court like a scion
by an embassy pool. I'm a thankless
bastard. One day I might pass gas incessantly,
publish a book on encephalitic buttocks,
and lead raids on alcoholic colonies with groups
of camouflaged prep school commandoes.
Pardon my arrogant vulgarity,
but I'm no sputtering quail:
I need a fucking stockbroker's cocktail,
I want a band to play my berserk epitaph,
for I have no catalogue of sins to conceal,
I'm only a curator of angst and zeal,
I'll bloom with respect as I exit
like a collection of ravens flying
through the juggernaut of qualms.
I'll bend down and pull the roots
from my native soil, I won't cost
you a pittance as you judge me cursing,
a human argument who chokes in rage,
a trolley of bones screeching to a dead halt.

Pattern ~ David Spicer

The redheaded gigolo ferried songs
from the bed of one bored goddess to another—
they inspired his razor wit and embroidered gut.
He chiseled their genitalia like
a psychopathic angel, leaping from any number
of horny sculptures to a tablecloth canvas in
his studio. Multi-talented, he preyed upon
their appreciations like a fluorescent rhododendron,
schemed to confront weaknesses
when they sipped Bordeaux and nibbled
cottage cheese with tomatoes. They desired him,
his self-portrait, but he snubbed that request,
informed them it was a tombstone
before the cancer or stroke. After
his camera plotted their gradual
dance into a topography of the disappeared,
he always raised polished eyebrows and added
a bra to his collection and shampooed one more wig.
He remembered his flames, from the Israeli
bus to the pondering eucalyptus,
and forever felt they'd gamble and return to him,
a pioneer with the cheating bomb
between his legs, but they didn't.
Except that lady singing the anthem, armed with a grin.

Request ~ David Spicer

I can't forgive my smug brains,
so how can I expect you to? If I had
the ice of an Irish billionaire
I'd hogtie you naked in a Kabuki museum,
have you arrested on the word
of rumors. I mingle in tatters
of pelvis-tango palaces,
a collection of incidents who wants
to propose to a smoke fiancé.
In this asylum, the doctor plays the Bolero
for us, his nicknamed racehorses:
Rhubarb, Cinnamon, Easy Money.
What can I do, slip away like a sardonic eel,
become a zealot condemning gospels,
or petition for my own acolyte?
I'm not even a trustee, or I'd vanish
like a vintage dissident, hide in the steeple
and devour hammers for breakfast.
I'm their centerpiece, a musky cur,
a spy with martyred ankles.
I'm tired of laughter, so come and get me.
I swear I'll love you like a nurse.

Promised Triptych ~ David Spicer

Bunny, a snarky communist from Budapest
with a temper, studied Scientology with me
in the cul-de-sac mansion off Ahab Street.
An epicure with a ruthless bikini,
she trained a magpie that moonlighted
as a flippant necromancer in a foulard vest.
She claimed he answered to Harpo and wasn't
a bumpkin. I knew his palaver remained
pompous. Sure, I was the seventh husband
in the tapestry of her cruise through tangles
of mascara and witty fevers,
and Harpo's rococo dance in an oak forest
behind lampposts served as bombast
for mea culpa digression. I dallied an orange,
promised a triptych he'd love, but he flew away
with the brunt of a buff dandy,
and Bunny revised a manifesto for comics
in jail. A phantom with spunk, she adored
Harpo and me without an infliction of pity.
Loved tactics pickled and diced
without a fee and sang that life is a rebus.
I remember a saint who danced in a soaked
trench coat to the beat of reggae,
elated she kept her name. The song's chorus
coaxed a new myth from her that slashed
the sunshine from the night's shallows.

Pillow Talk After The Moulin Rouge ~ David Spicer

Tattooed Tatiana from Hollywood
branded me an asshole who smirked
like an Eskimo riding a hog.
I called her a petite libertine who gasped
like a lilac sandpiper. She baked
a soufflé laced with scotch and teardrops
before we flicked our ostrich-feather tongues.
Her passion beat me with a rubber hammer
and the grace of a doe-eyed maid. Divorced
after the dilemma of marriages, we gossiped
in a backseat battlefield of cremated mischief.
Our karate words kissed each other's salty bellies.
She called me a spineless mama's boy
and I returned the favor with *gutless goose*.
Our lips tossed the dozens with the vengeance
of addicts. Midnight hobnobbed around us.
We agreed we had no peers among coeds,
wives, or twerps who shopped for buttons to push,
and hated bosses of protégé cults sipping
ice in demitasse. I chose my favorite
tattoos between her shoulder blades, a violet
wolf hunt and a floozy kissing a calendar.
She deemed me a sweaty impresario,
a long-tongued putz who killed the night
like a tourist wearing brand new corduroys.

Venice In Furs ~ David Spicer

More ego than talent, clever but not quite enough
cornrowed Venice in furs assessed my words and me,
an icon for nobody but the camera of lame wit.
Loathe to stand behind a dais and loan an ashtray,
I steered clear of her tongue's tai chi, a virus of words
pandemic to the folie à deux of epithets of woo.
I forgive the abuse of your peony dagger, Venice,
your heart a bloated tin of red tears.
I love the sabotage of gouache botany.
Our affair on a train with the midnight chick
was our scar and spade. *Shut the blinds*, you advised,
and I'll serve a lunch of raw yeast in your pot.
I buried it long ago for such occasions, painted rich
fishermen on canvas in the studio and left a tablet
on the outskirts of the rail yard. Her haven tumbled.
Outside the wool lining of furs, I watched
the doorman blow cobwebs away and say
The troops are here, sir. You can play polo now.

DAVID SPICER *has, over the years and in pursuit of*
the word, worked as a paper boy, dishwasher, bottle
loader, record warehouser, carpet roll dragger, burger
flopper, ditch digger, weather observer, furniture
mover, Manpower flunky, gas pumper, bookseller,
tutor, 11th and 12th grader babysitter, magazine and
book editor and publisher, typesetter, proofreader,
librarian's assistant, carney barker, chocolate twister,
and artist's model. He is the author of one full-length
collection of poems, Everybody Has a Story, *and four*
chapbooks, plus eight unpublished manuscripts. He is
the former editor of raccoon, Outlaw, *and Ion Books*
and has published in the usual slicks, non-slicks, and
online journals.

Far away ~ Yariv Zerbib

Millions of penguins
Took over a vast area of the Mediterranean
A Norwegian police commissioner intervened
I urged him to stop

After all

It happened naturally.

In the universe ~ Yariv Zerbib

I was so happy to see
A flock of whales
Crossing the sky
To

Infinity.

Sunday morning ~ Yariv Zerbib

I love coffee
Especially when the seeds arrive from planet Venus
They have a fragrance

As such

That causes shivers.

Daydream ~ Yariv Zerbib

On the middle of the path
An armadillo appeared from my shadow
And said

The secret lies in water.

What a mess ~ Yariv Zerbib

The Beetles began to erode galaxies
One after the other
Flying Fish tried to prevent this from happening

And everything

Because one dead moon.

Venom ~ Yariv Zerbib

The snake that slithered inside my body
Shed his skin and felt
For his prey
Now

Beware all city mice.

Marlene My Love ~ Yariv Zerbib

The distance between the two universes is enormous
The eagle walked away from responsibility
If only the crow were there

I knew

It could have made history here.

A spark in the ground ~ Yariv Zerbib

I dug as deep as I could
The centipede decided that enough was enough
There are too many spying birds

Clearly

Gold-saturated bedrock.

The petting zoo ~ Yariv Zerbib

There are too many planets inside the helmet
You will need a cannon
Just to loosen the atmosphere

Know

The truth is always dark.

Butterflies Valley ~ Yariv Zerbib

The fear that something was going to happen
Placed billions of Meerkats on their feet
Buildings collapsed

In the end

It was a supernova in a neighboring galaxy.

Back from vacation ~ Yariv Zerbib

Many stingrays returned after a long stay on the moon
Why did they not stay longer? I thought
The view is spectacular there

Probably

An electron wave blocked the sun.

Fortune ~ Yariv Zerbib

I sold all the assets on planet Pluto
I'm rich
I can now

Live

As ants live.

YARIV ZERBIB is a short story author, novelist, and poet. He lives on planet Jupiter, works as a junior scientist at the Institute for the Study of Caves. His work appears in uutpoetry mag. His first two books, the first a novella and the second a collection of poems, will soon be published. You can visit him at his blog http://psikpub.tumblr.com/ or on facebook https://www.facebook.com/yariv.zerbib

yours, in sintering ~ Scherezade Siobhan

we are horizoned through the city's veneered metallurgy -
clouds idling in copper-bordered cobwebs

& rain is a language loosened into the untied
shoelaces of ash-freckled neighborhood boys

a plashet, a game of marbles, a caravan of tinnitus

i bring you to the kiln of my country
where the midas gold of skin turns

to a dusk of woodcutters waking in the red
sycamores. we sleep on the temple floor, dream

of the stolen idols arising in an antimony
of war-hooded serpents. the thunderstorm

shaking the gulmohar trees to an unflagging epilepsy.
the lava-colored flowers spat out in their ember-teeth

as the night knocks on rockpaths; an old blacksmith
& the iron under your fingernails flickering its oil burner,

a translucence of wings on dying fireflies; molten
as an undressed volcano; a minefield of catharsis

Be my firefighter's red - I ~ Scherezade Siobhan

after andrew varnon's "be my sherpa"

be my ether hawking astronaut, my clam digger
through pisces, the zodiac drawl i can barely winnow

what if there is a larger payoff at the end?
be my auditor of augury
my crystal ball and my calculator

I know there are pyramid texts underneath your eyelids
be my sophomore pharaoh
my guerrilla underground,
my crossbow, my archer's locus
my ageless shrine on the sand

be my excathedra, my bespectacled pharmacist, my
 placebo
playing hopscotch with the prescription
my dusk folding its breath into an origami swan
my high heeled canyons snaking through andalusia
my lace of paddy fields murmured into the outskirts
 of saigon

be my jungian scarab, my objet petit, my electra
 complex, my psychedelic Eros,
my treadmill trained catharsis
be my orison for antidote

be my fire exit flower garden, my petite paw of
 peonies, my slender render of a
rosemary sprig, my terrace swing, my through-to-
 christmas spring fling

be my pianissimo outré, my bario gig,
my theolonius monk blended in a blue agave swig

be my mezzotinted mountaintop, my rope, my rappel
be my bolt-chopped boulder
my deadman anchor for the snow to nurse
my cordelette coupled in chapter & verse

my petrarchan sonnet, my herculean harmony
my bird-dog trumpet of the iamb
be my midnight oil to burn
be my spare key under the welcome mat
be my greyhound window seat
a tottering bus ride, a childhood home to return

be my outlier, my doyen of debonair, my
sparkplug electrocuting the humbug

be my ceteris paribus, my single-minded symmetry
the foxhole to my cavalier atheist
my temple bell
my secret chapel

be my penalty shot, my matchpoint,
my love all grand slam

be my scuba stroll, my guardian angel aqualung,
be my matrix of the great barrier reef,
my octopus spread out like sea wrack
my mussel mystery
my continental aphrodisiac

be my guiding principle
my Armageddon chess
be my synapse in the seismograph
be my voltaic earth in a belly laugh
be my underpinning stab in the dark
my lava blood, my macadam's arc

be voynich manuscript
the iron gall ink in my cipher drift

be my ship in the bottle
my coy coastline, my nightingale in contralto
be my lemon sass beatbox,
my ghetto acoustics

be my short straw, be my reluctant karma
be my godly calculus, my lucky draw
be my seven courtyards in the countryside
be my stone inn, my glossary of orchids
my basilica made of candle wax

be these moments of muscle memory. be my everyday.
be my compound interest of all the leap years.
be my hussars of an antique idolatry.

be these things. be mine. i'm drawing out my
framework from the river fog. i am making myself
readable, sightseer. i am asking for an education of
hands from someone who knows how to touch like
water and wait like the sky. this is how you can be
the bedrock riot of roots - aren't i your branch? your
fluctuating profit. this is what you will remember of
the past. the quasar is an incomplete paragraph.
dark matter is the cosmic cradle.
it births each universe with its own siamese twin. i
am telling you this. all of this we already are. each
soft-shell axis, each harvested consonant. fall, dive
deep.

be my wildcard underdog, my spry spell
be my sign language settlements
my alphabet apartment blocks
my road to raid, my road to read
be my gray-haired signposts
my racked up trans-atlantic miles
my morning deer breakfasting on the basil stalks

be my kiss between light & lightning.
be my glimmering, whispering, ravishing, lingering,
 sparkling and shivering

be my unapologetic debate
be my lionhearted apostate
be my perfectly broken taboo
be table for two, my quick on trigger
satire, my one man troupe of har-har!

be my enter your spouse's name in this box, my
 emergency phone number, my
makeshift chef, carpenter, plumber

be my always rules the roost on the list of all last
 dialed calls
be my shadow's dress in old stairwells & movie halls

be that string of feats: where you walk, run, jump
into burning buildings, put your whole body through
the blaze, wear ash like an old coat & still come out,
not a single thread of that skin's gossamer on
tenterhooks.

be my wake up. be my come to bed. be my wide
open evening walk through Champs-Élysées.

and i am finally old now. i can begin as late as we like.

SCHEREZADE   SIOBHAN   *is   an   Indo-Roma
storyteller, psychologist and Jungian scarab. Her first
collection   of   poetry   entitled   "Bone   Tongue"   was
released   by   Thought   Catalog   Books   in   2015.   Her
second   collection,   "Father,   Husband",   was   published
by   Salò   Press   in   2015.   Her   writing   has   appeared
and/or is forthcoming in* Queen Mob's, TMO Magazine,
Cordite   Poetry   Review,   Winter   Tangerine,   Potluck,
Electric   Cereal,   tNYPress,   Fruita   Pulp,   Harpoon
Review,   DIAGRAM,   Wasafiri,   Timber   Literary   Journal
*and others. Her lineage ensures that she is perennially
nomadic and immersed in fernweh.*

The Valise ~ Jake Hostetter

You see I am at the table. My manner and how I have set the table are suggestive of a scenario you will recognize as unlikely but nonetheless entertain. Perhaps what I have done is prepared you dinner. However, there is no food, no silverware on the table. There is a candle, and where your plate would be there is my carob brown valise, a briefcase especially tailored for wine though far from restricted to transportation of Merlot.

So perhaps what I have done is tried to make you dinner. Tried. There was a failure, the experience of humiliation, which I relived over and over again when I saw the grotesquerie I prepared in lieu of dinner. And unable to bear the humiliation, what I have done is scrape the grotesquerie I made for you into a section of my valise, once upon a time fashioned for a bottle of exquisite wine, and, now, forced to stomach pigswill. And I have shut the valise. And I have latched the valise, clamped the valise because the pigswill, as a crime against Nature herself, was a danger to come alive, escape, attack.

In spite of it all, I made you something. *I made you something!* And here I am about to present you with a gift in my valise, a special delivery. A special delivery from hell. It's a scenario I call, "The Grotesquerie For Dinner."

Another scenario: You arrive wearing a ghoulish opera mask made of ivory. I ask, "Are you really so hideous?" You nod and approach the table, nearing my carob brown valise. Unnaturally, I am nervous and I laugh, saying, "No average bag now is it, my valise?" You nod. You only nod. I implore you to speak. I have no need to see your face, but words I need. *Words, a word, sir! Please!*

Finally, you respond, your voice more from your

chest than your mouth. You say you are thinking of a train. On this train there will be an act, an act regarded by the authorities as criminal. I ask, "A murder?"

"A mystery," you nearly growl. The key to solving the mystery will be found inside. You will whisper, "Inside the valise."

*

A moon's orbit ago, back before you and I began our communications, I was approaching the dead end of my intrigue with Mr. Furr, my employer. The affair hatched from what was internally, I imagined, a pea-sized expression of my curiosity over the man's mask. Business attire for Mr. Furr went above mere formality. It surpassed my own admitted opulence, my Hounds Tooth Suit. Everyday Mr. Furr wore a black wool balaclava, one of the sportier masks seen generally on ski resorts or freezie-popped terrorists. Indeed, Mr. Furr was cold, strangled discourse with him quite chilling. Naturally, my co-employees felt compelled to improvise layers when around him, ensconcing themselves in bubble wrap and whatever other packaging material was on hand at the time, anything to compensate for the sudden drop in temperature, the chill. Mr. Furr made us all feel cold. But was the man self-aware enough to be as affected by himself, his mask in place to combat chronically low body temperature? Or was the mask on Mr. Furr's face there to cover for something else, something horrible – burns, perhaps? None of us at the office had ever seen him without the mask.

The face-mask had three holes: Two for the eyes and one for the mouth, the latter of which I one day recognized as a sign of compelling life. Yes, it is perverse as all that, and the depravity I plan on expelling here.

Our personal liaison began with a knock, his unintelligible response and my brusque entry.

Whoops, I surprised Mr. Furr while he spooned himself cocoa pudding, his face-mask, sadly for me, still on, his mask always on. Devious little spoon, I thought, docking in what, to me in the context of the greater office, and then, his inner sanctum, his mouth, increasingly warranted, in a way that I could taste, the status of uncharted terrain. He was hungry, hungry for meaning, for life, and ready. He was ready, I could taste it, then, to bargain for a warmer, sweeter life with me. I was that hot. Apparently, that hot to trot.

He started ordering me to his sanctum over the telephone. *Ring, ring*. "Master beckons, Daniel," or some such crap designed to remind me of my more canine attributes and the associated slavishness demanded of a retriever dog. Still, I would report to him, marching indignantly through his door, slam, theater for the co-employees in whom I hoped to inspire bravery. By then Mr. Furr would have cleared most or all of the objects from his desk, sheets of paper carefully strewn on the floor, papers for puppy on the albine bear pelt, a nearby space-heater, smoking as the result of forced contact with a paper stamped "classified", Mr. Furr out from behind his desk already sucking up the intended smoke with a vacuum hose. He didn't address me until he was back at his desk, in his chair, the vacuum under the desk where I could not see the silver canister and hose, not while standing. Then out would come his briefcase on the desk. Unlatching the briefcase filled Mr. Furr with barely contained obscenity, evidence of which, the wantoness, I heard in his nasty little phlegmatic moans, similar in sound and yet opposite to the vacuum, occasionally left droning beneath his desk, his face-mask on still, of course. Mr. Furr's smile displayed an unnatural number of tiny teeth, well-lacquered, shining, in defiance of expectations. And, inside of his briefcase: Two bananas.

The first time Mr. Furr revealed the bananas in his briefcase, he immediately set a place for me across from him, the proposed scenario: a brunch. Only, I wouldn't be joining M. Furr, exactly, at the desk. My intended seat was on the floor near the hindquarters of the polar pelt. Mr. Furr spent harrowing time up North, I assumed, where aspects of his character frostbit then rotted off altogether. I ventured that scenario as my hypothesis for how Mr. Furr's sensitivity dulled and damned. At the ass of a bludgeoned polar bear, he had placed a red plastic dog bowl. Brunch! Help myself, at first, sitting where I could see not his masked face, but his pointed shoes, black spandex in place of socks, the hem of the pants, and the silver vacuum canister and hose beneath his desk, the carpet a murk. *No hands allowed. Stand. Pick banana up with mouth. Face the door. Squat. Now on my knees. Drop banana in dog bowl on the pelt on the floor. Beg Master help Puppy peel banana.*

Here, I will interrupt the bananas to prepare you for a turn in the story, a transformation in myself that begs an explanation I still find hard to articulate. To start things how about a general point of inquiry: Do you realize I can be quite sick? I believe you have an idea, though perhaps it the wrong idea, a kinder sort of idea. I'll wryly suggest an alternative approach. Acquaint yourself with depravity, initially, just a bit. If, then, you find you are paralyzed by the fear of where your mind will go next, unsure about the physics of inertia, I say talk about the stars, astronomy. What's the moon doing? Because what triggers my metamorphosis is an everyday wonder, Aren't I livid about injustice? The consequences bring tears to my eyes when my suddenly inflated, harried brawn busts an inseam, the lunatic outrage inside of me outside again.

"Do you observe where Master eats the banana?"

At a desk. Mr. Furr ate his banana sitting at his desk, where, from the floor, if I stayed kneeled, looking where he commanded I look, I could hear only the salival chewing.

"Where does slave eat the banana?" He tossed his peel at the dog bowl in case I hadn't noticed, and, one day, when the peel missed, landing astride the red plastic rim, but mostly on the matted white of the polar pelt, I recognized the gesture for the ugly, haphazard act it was, a climactic bit of carelessness from Mr. Furr. The outrage I suffered for the polar pelt was enough to rocket me to Outer Space, the moon, a boom, all inflated larger in the mind's eye until it overshadowed all else and I become a werewolf, a real life werewolf. A man-wolf, I seem to be standing in the shadow of a bright, ambiguous force in the dark of the sky, a sudden dark room, much too present and mine to be the night with the moon, but like the moon. Me, a howl away from awareness that again, again, I am not fully a man, but a monster. I was on my knees and then, almost, crawling on and clawing the ceiling.

"I am no retriever dog." I told him that and he clapped, pronouncing me his Wehrwolfe. He tendered another awful smile, nothing more. He hadn't taken off his mask yet. The imbalance between us compelled me near enough to lose my job, plus smell a string of banana preserved in the Mister's molars, his tiny teeth rounded at the heads like thimbles, his tongue thin and patched white.

"In the future," I told him, "I'd prefer eating on a chair with you at your desk."

He understood, alright. "Ah, yes," I remember him saying. "A Wehrwolfe, a fighter, a soldier." From then on, we agreed that I would set my own briefcase on the desk alongside his. Furthermore, I would refer to my briefcase by its proper designation, no matter how severe the unfamiliarity that term may breed. "Valise," I said, introducing it to his desk. "Here is my carob brown valise, a kind of briefcase especially tailored for French wine."

Acquiescing to the idea surprisingly pleased Mr. Furr who, simulating a hello with his own briefcase while it faced my valise, half-closed and then opened it. "Very nice to meet you, Herr Valise." A rather forced response, yes, but still the abrasive whimsicality bucked my idea about his imagination, which I'd begun to believe had the approximate dimensions of a bondage basement.

The time that followed would be our happiest together, Mr. Furr and me, those next few seconds. Naturally, he ruined the bliss by promptly describing for me what would be our rotting new, but old, routine: *No hands allowed. Pick banana up with mouth. Drop banana in valise. Permission to speak, General. Permission granted. Help Wehrwolfe peel banana.* I seized it with my hands, the banana. Do imagine my graceful motion in snatching the banana from "General" Furr's briefcase and jamming it, on the floor, in the sanded soft maw of the polar pelt.

Outside his sanctum's door, I made a vow: *Demystification of the masked!* Words that I marked on my weekly planner. Monday, Monday, Monday. Goals for a week of Mondays: Strip the General. He had seen the dog, then the wolf, in me, and now it was his turn to unmask. The next day, I insisted, "The mask. Show me yours." I even gestured at him with a banana, which broke some rule or other, him trembling, him swatting the banana out of my hands, and me letting the fruit fall to the floor, just shy of the polar pelt's ass. That time, Mr. Furr retrieved the banana. But he took aim at me with the banana, Mr. Furr, at once, fiercely displeased and joyous. He said, "Bang, bang." Then, his barely actualized wheeze, the sudden diversion to his vacuum cleaner beneath the desk, or so I thought. Instead, the opening of a bottom drawer.

As my employer, you see, Mr. Furr had performed his own job outstandingly, training me to take it and take it until what it was asked I take was a bullet, quite literally. When he unhunched from his desk, it wasn't with the vacuum, but with a pistol, an actual, *Bang bang*, pistol, he brandished before placing it in his opened briefcase on his desktop. "Nien to hand privileges," he said. "Pick up pistol only with mouth."

I remember laughing. I laughed so hard I howled. His face-mask caved, Mr. Furr's tiny teeth vanishing, the hole for his mouth dark, and he repeated the bit about the pistol. *Pick up pistol, pick up*, the redundancy hammering my understanding of his true intent right on down to the floor where I studied the matted polar pelt, vacuumed clean as snow. *How did I get there?* Mr. Furr puzzled me further in vocal description of the pistol, the caliber and alloy of bullet, the origin of the firearm, etcetera. Once I, the Wehrwolfe, opened my mouth to the head of the pistol, he, too, would display true vulnerability, his face-mask, off it'd come.

I said something about our working relationship coming to an end. He lurched for the gun. I grabbed it first. They may not be cat-like, but lupine reflexes can be hair-trigger. He demanded I return the gun, sentimental value, fathers upon fathers upon very dead fathers. "You, Mr. Furr are hideous," and I pointed the gun at him. "Mask on or off, I see all of you." I said, "You are weaker than you anticipated. Remind yourself of the vulnerability you cannot conceal before you menace me again."

He spat as I backed out of the sanctum. Before I closed the door, he wished me all the best. I expected him sooner, but it took a full week before I heard his wheeze again, smelling the wrong sweetness of his pudding. While I was sitting at my cubicle, I heard the wheeze, the pistol already in my lap, waiting for such encroachment. I propped the gun on my shoulder and nudged it away, the wheeze at my ear, then behind a flop wall, then further. I didn't have to turn to face him to convince Mr. Furr he was little other than a figurehead now, and a damned one at that. I dared him to be redundant. "Adversaries!" he shrilled, retreating to his sanctum. But there, in his sanctum, his little cube, he stayed, while I set to work probing the technology and my co-employees in the greater office for work elsewhere. Until I find what I am looking for, I keep the pistol in my valise, the valise at my side wherever I go.

In other words, I have baggage, some more than figurative baggage. Mine qualified, how about you? Do not leave me feeling unbalanced.

*Whilst **JAKE HOSTETTER** was earning his masters in Fiction Writing at Penn State, Glimmer Train recognized my story, "GFG" as a semi-finalist in their annual Best New Writer contest. Most recently, MCB Quarterly accepted his story "Jellybang" for publication in their up-and-coming volume devoted to Queer Speculative Fiction.*

Slumber Party Panic ~ Zachary Cosby

A cloud of smoke shaped like a skull. Help me look as young and alive as you. A heart that craves sugar. I kick and kick and kick you apart. A pinata still breathing. Everyone loves slumber parties. With a shovel you scream. Never tell anyone about this. You put your hand near my mouth. You are amazed. My arms can stretch out and across the room. They stretch out the window and into the night. I do not know what they are touching. Ooooh, says everyone. Oooooh. We beat a pinata to death. We live inside a giant vending machine. When a mouth opens, teeth. This is messed up, you say, but sweet. You can break a promise but you can't call back death.

The Jiggler ~ Zachary Cosby

We are walking in a place where the hills they stretch forever. The trees are either very large or very small or very far away. I feel like singing and dancing. I feel like taking you home, like splitting my toothbrush in half so you can use half, like playing until we blow out the candles. I eat and eat dark red grapes like swallowing tiny computers. You push a mechanical grape into my mouth, but what's the worst that could happen? What's the most a body could hurt? This room is spinning. I am vomiting red from every hole. There is red vomit on your shirt and in your head. You are crying on the floor and thinking of the way it feels to throw handfuls of pearls into an ocean. I can fix this.

Ricardio The Heart Guy ~ Zachary Cosby

I have two stones instead of eyes. This thing wrapped around my face like a mask, that is a snow tipped mountain. I am standing in the corner of the party and dancing science. Would you like to meet all my new emotions? Over there, sitting on the rooftop with our knees tucked in. I think our guts are a little naive. Throw me in the dumpster, until no one has to feel jealous anymore.

What Is Life ~ Zachary Cosby

I clap my wet wooden hands. I press my nose to your nose. We do this in ways that feel neverending. There is another moment for the feeling. Please please warn me next time. Please warn me if you want to go. I lay in bed and touch soft things. I rub my fingers against other fingers. How often do you feel like an innocent bystander? Watching in so much awe. When I open a door I see you. You can touch my open face as an explorer walking through sadness or a field with two quiet dogs. Can I finish a poem in the imagination of clouds? Can I talk?

Business Time ~ Zachary Cosby

When we are together, we become a new kind of global warming. We wander through the arctic with flamethrowers strapped to our backs and melt every glacier into nothing. I climb on top of a very old glacier and burn away the ice around my feet. You make a dozen snowmen and burn their faces off. You burn and burn their faces until they are nothing but a dozen tiny swimming pools, and then we go swimming a dozen times. We cheer as giant chunks of ice fall into the sea. I hold your hand as hot water splashes your face. We don't know how to sleep so instead of sleeping, we eat gallons of shaved ice until our mouths go blue and numb, and then we hunt polar bears to extinction. You tell me that you hear millions of people all screaming at once, somewhere faraway in the south. They sound just like a peach being crushed under the weight of an enormous machine.

Freak City ~ Zachary Cosby

We are walking and sometimes touching each other's faces. Sometimes I lay on the ground like a bicycle. I can't even bend my eyes into my own head. I miss the way suns form, the explosions. A pair of blue jeans from yesterday and the smallest of open questions. I made a blanket sewn from forest hangovers to keep. Being in a body seems like a battle I cannot win. No one is afraid any longer. I met a man laughing on the hilltops. He asked: is it possible to stop for breath?

ZACHARY COSBY lives in Portland, Oregon. He is 24 years old.

UNEXPECTED DEVELOPMENT ~ T.D.Typaldos

Inside his phallus
You can find world's navel
The troughs throw up the moving embryos
The insects fly all around the iceberg's top
Afternoon walk into the gloomy garden of
    a perennial resignated peal

At night the statues obtain breath-life-voice
They step off the pedestals and spit heads open

ΑΠΡΟΣΔΟΚΗΤΗ ΕΞΕΛΙΞΗ ~ T.D.Typaldos

Είναι στον φαλλό του μέσα
Του κόσμου ο ομφαλός
Οι γούρνες ξερνούν τα έμβρυα της κίνησης
Τα έντομα πετούν ολόγυρα στου παγόβουνου
    την κορφή
Μεσημεριανός περίπατος στην αυλή της ζοφερής
    αιωνόβιας ρίψασπις κωδωνοκρουσίας

Τις νύχτες παίρνουν τ' αγάλματα πνοή-ζωή-φωνή
Απ' τα βάθρα τους κατεβαίνουν κι ανοίγουν κεφάλια

MATHEMATICAL EQUATION ~ T.D.Typaldos

A leg
As a rectangle
A hand
As a triangle with equal sides
A head
As a cube with a right angle
A leg
A hand
A head
All together
Within a tomb

ΜΑΘΗΜΑΤΙΚΗ ΕΞΙΣΩΣΗ ~ T.D.Typaldos

Ένα πόδι
Ορθογώνιο παραλληλόγραμμο
Ένα χέρι
Τρίγωνο ισοσκελές
Ένα κεφάλι
Κύβος με ορθή γωνία
Ένα πόδι
Ένα χέρι
Ένα κεφάλι
Όλα μαζί
Σ' ένα τάφο

MEA CULPA ~ T.D.Typaldos

Arachinds
Obstructions
Spits
Blasphemies
Into an
Aspirin's
Little
Pussy

MEA CULPA ~ T.D.Typaldos

Αραχνοειδείς
Αποφράξεις
Φτύνουν
Βλασφήμιες
Στο
Μουνί
Μιας
Ασπιρίνης

WATCHING THE EXCITEMENT ARISING FROM YOUR BODY ~ T.D.Typaldos

Watching the excitement arising from your body
I burst my anger upon you
The wrath of an oppressed god
An hermaphrodite god
With genitals
From a shell's torn fan
From a corner's loose rhyme
Behind my ear
A tusk grows
You, my Pleasure and my Curse
I, your Love and your Death
Over the bone of your third eye
Fata Morgana sharpens the drumming
    of the profundis cunnus
I am the Prophet of Obscurity
You are the Consummation of The Last Planet

ΠΑΡΑΚΟΛΟΥΘΩ ΤΗΝ ΕΞΑΨΗ ΠΟΥ ΑΠΟΡΡΕΕΙ ΑΠ΄ ΤΟ ΚΟΡΜΙ ΣΟΥ ~ T.D.Typaldos

Παρακολουθώ την έξαψη που απορρέει απ΄ το κορμί
σου
Ξεσπάω επάνω σου την οργή μου
Την οργή ενός θεού καταπιεσμένου
Ενός ερμαφρόδιτου θεού
Με γεννητικά όργανα
Από όστρακο σχισμένης βεντάλιας
Από γωνίες σαθρής ομοιοκαταληψίας
Πίσω απ΄ το αυτί μου
Ένας χαυλιόδοντας φυτρώνει
Εσύ η Ηδονή κι η Κατάρα μου
Εγώ ο Έρωτας κι ο Θάνατός σου
Πάνω στο κόκαλο του τρίτου σου οφθαλμού
Η Fata Morgana την τυμπανοκρουσία ακονίζει
    του de profundis cunnus
Εγώ ο Προφήτης της Αφάνειας
Εσύ η Ολοκλήρωση του Τελευταίου Πλανήτη

*Born in 1975 under the name Thomas Petropoulos,
however, when he writes, the name alters to
T.D.TYPALDOS thus acquiring absolute freedom that
reality deprives. He has participated in a collection of
distinctive poems, in the latest issue of a magazine
publication of the Surrealist Group of Athens
KLIDONAS with a poem of his, and has published two
surrealistic narratives in the forms of e-books.*

Years in a Seahorse ~ Zachary Scott Hamilton

Life in a Seahorse

|i.| balloons

YEARS SPENT IN A SEAHORSE, padding for our beautiful mutation symphony, to keep away vampirism, BALLOONS ARE IN THE TELEVISION My mind is still a balloon full of helium, a propped usnea, our bed soft shale, or glow in the dark. I am wandering through shale, I store a few balloons, and a dream, (still marbled paper for tuesday, with neon, with a baseball field look on my face) in your home. / I

straightened out my shoulders, sewing with hands, even the electric, neon, soap, all of the way crystal. I found a glass of water in the forest, filled my wandering legs with orchids, and vines, I was a doctor, hunting arms. Then to tug boat, a thin, blue Christ, I thread it, the gift, with my dithering ape hangers /

When I arrive at your residence,
seven seconds passes, eats wooden
doorway like dinosaur, using
topics like healing with garlic,
shears to party with, the state of
the union, the same toys as radios
and paintings, homelessness in the
inner city, these make up an hour
for me, and the gift is left
abandoned in your living room. A
few weeks passes./
I figure if I sit down with you, and
bring glyphs into your eyes, on
the oldest animal school bus
and the spinning through sunday,
summer waterfall, streetcar,
Leontine, send mail from God, --
I've forgotten about it--the wind
might bring a chill, unsettling. The
water had become all glitter, it
knew nothing else.
Happy Thanksgiving, the card
reads.
A dinosaur runs up out of
nowhere, a mcdonalds wrapper
becomes monster, on Bordeaux,
silent glass, and the rest of Berlin
unfolds with us. Six seconds (you
seem pretty sure) are going
through equations of creating five
seconds stuffed in a box with a
key. /

MIDNIGHT HAWK, four Earthworms burrow three holes in the cabinetry, in the flower print. AH, They shake their tail feathers, we're under a willow tree, they walk like dinosaurs, Vine dreams like tendrils, a vertical ladder, tide painted sun~ then the education. / The birds swim across the water, reflecting the sunlight in their wake, the waves sparkle, and shimmer. They gather amongst themselves. A silent, plastic becomes a visual monster on Marengo- Spectacles

Healing from freeze-frame with two black hats, that float underwater, upside down in a mirror boat, split in screens, two each side of a dark brown mule, passing Arc st. quarters, spectacles digging glass with their new album, like spiders, hospital and a queens hand, glove-handkerchief umbrellas flying over the ocean; one, spinning nowhere, one in the rainbow. / Middletown, turning a record beneath the needle claw, his wife closes herself in eyelashes. Leprechauns climb out of old pottery all around the floating room. Middletown is a strange place, each bit of burning aroma wanders like tourists to the sea, the passage is in ocher locks of lichen, like arms foraging for a thousand breakfasts, in a claw foot tub, before moon and flame, bathing in leaves on the webs of sleep near the eaves of a French impersonator, Godfrey, with rockets in her dreams, large green eyes, and delicate hands. Godfrey, who flirts with a tv remote. Her finger nails glitter in the static, dreams switching channels, static as she sleeps./ Closely now, trimmed in a white dance of basil lakes, and parasols that leak out speakers, the boats turn green. / The algae, laughing, goat for halloween! Waking (A. in glove), (A. in goat) eating cakes. Godfrey samples small locks of her keyboard with knife-point algebra. The road lets in floating military backpacks, to wire with soldering, and children and Leaf the childrens world, just left heart beat, just playback oxygen, Oxen wanderlust beneath them. /

|ii.| wednesday

(E a) in glitter, Face the symmetrical furniture, the chandeliers, the jacket, the green, neon clock. The angel Auriel Godfrey does, she makes sure the favorite pair of color swatch eyes, the best way to the nose, eating cakes in the identical Wednesday, dancing on the slides with a hundred years to kill is in the letter, and on its way to the post office. / The green light of the men's auras play soccer in a galaxy swirl, they are toy soldiers in mint Gelato. I am curious, humane, sheltered in scarves. I have grown a lot of wings from maple, and New York City. I even found a place for the past in my gift to Auriel, and I will have a healthy fear of those green toys, jangled in keys next to the passage of twilight. I join handmade letters from cardboard, kiss under heavens, float to shore, as Zachary.

|iii.| Friday

A GERMAN DOLL At the felt sleeve of
the cosmos, the Catalina, rafts, and
sailing Eucla cod, the Elvers feeding on
atoms, and suspended in animations so
the Danio can gorge on tv commercials
from the airport.
There are nine awkward turns to go,
thanks to the iceberg, angel Auriel
Godfrey'sfirst frozen mammoths appear
in the story of a frozen bridge, and
reflecting ponds, the snow suits, and
warm tongues leaking over in the
octopus sculpture, hanging off the
boat. Blueberries.

|iv.| vinyl

BLUE INK, Swerves into a hat, into a
white whale, a bird, throwing glitter, and
showing off a slow motion glowing retina
tin can, sews past the boat. Sewing
machine spit, conditioner lathered foam
noise. Lurching on a wire, a maple figure,
woven all blackberry nightmare under the
stitch of winding doors unfolding behind
it. Sculptures are quickly made of hair by
my crew, and the tempo is set for songs,
and gold furniture, and we rewind the
tape.
She finds the gift, and opens it in her
living room.
Slow motion, a man in the corner dressed
in scuba gear puts on a record. Intricate
bird cages, roosters out of the gift wrap.
"The sky was cancelled today, but
infinity is still marbled for tuesday." The
record whispers.
Auriel's tears of joy leak to the carpet,
and she kisses the card in her hands,
goodnight.

|v.| Tuesday

A No. Of Dynamic Secrets, BUSES, Two
queens and eight hats from scuba gear
guy's lungs, shallow in the mind of an
abracadabra tuesday. joining two sets of
hair in a long braid of whimpering
orgasm quartets, he follows angel Auriel
Godfrey through the hurried juniper solar
system, which won plaid and dusk, a fine
ghost draws with a white house, and
awoken with stick around like necklaces,
of course. Juniper is a small galaxy, the
roots are rooms sweating down the bright
handlebars, a dinosaur, the lenses.
Abracadabra! ropes and ribbon, futures
long, joining coastal, kinky brown
ligaments, juicing roses, weekend after
weekend. SHE TAKES OFF HIS
FLIPPERS! takes down the scuba mask,
Understand, this is the need to be held in
secret, all these flurries are distortion
wheels if midnight in Texas, I lay under
that chandelier turnkey, at 11 Christmas
bulbs, turned over, gorgeous boats in the
willow trees floaty aboveground, I am
closing my eyes, juniper trees line the
shore, and Ariel makes love to the scuba
dubba, VISTA! Elaborated chambers of
her body take 200 tetras, October 30th,
and not a human face, but a momentum
to land in "moment umbrella." Ethereal,
and steering the passage, arm in arm to
cavities. SHE keeps eye contact in her
hand like ingredients for diamonds in a
faith pocket, and dusk (a healthy
relationship between her and the long
drive away) saves my life to search a PhD
in library science. In my mind is helium,
and I feel the gorgeous, marble entry to
abandoned houses, all around me.
WANTED for latching onto a museum

like a tick. Chanelle comes in waves, shifts a satellite radio to worm hole. These two are fucking In a depth of yarn, lengthy hearts remodeling the universe for a canoe, Just P. M. Creek, apples chanting strawberries.

Ariel says

Dawn, you look lovely.

He says

Grow god inside mismatched, any roomy reward. I've forgotten the make up, the sweaters. He thinks in terms so tediously inscribed in the mirror, and wakes eating pino colada cake. Roped in roots is the world, unfolding polyamorous WAVES, Humans nesting in flat tires, free box clothes, in a frozen water fall, beneath an iced over maze. Dmitri -- who emerges dainty, (fully equipped kitchen in his hands,) time traveling with his knife collection -- Dmitri's fingers cut at the hair of sleep group no.5, 7, and 23, handling the tissue paper moon as delicate as the hair, below him, right before breakfast.

|vi.| Sunday

He BUTTONS up the dark coma, pours syrup from little glass bottles, pours red mouths this early in the house. I, version three hundred, have personally served benadryl to this Sickness for a very long time. I've been With the result there and weaving whistles to Irish wingspan, angelica, rosaries spinning in the home! My fingers are like ropes this morning, and your fingers are like Rosemary bundles lapped in 1965 waves. A doll comes now, so galactic it unravels a girlfriend naked onto the wooden floors, and our window sill. Auriel!?

|Vii.| OLD HIGHWAY

Over, in the venus fly trap, long, black finger-nail-needles, 10mg xanax prescriptions, and a shit pipe - New York job, I am number 12 in a room of eyeliner, cover up, and lipstick.
Four of the windows are my white sleeved waiters, they come in and go. Underground, beneath a cherry tree root, behind a red oak door, dancing to the foot stickers, dance by number, and a map tacked in the back of the room, I've no comparisons with myself as number 53, number 20, number 18. The numbers, filmed behind fog that play on reels of dream before the butterflies, eyelids, boxes of computer parts, broken fans, torn out hard drives, they have been left here, standing between this static, built above ground, in the sky, they've turned New York into ass gymnasiums, (on the one hand, I can literally fork lift mashed pieces of the static inside of a television apart from that skyline,) on the other hand, sweep pill bottles, oh, from the mountain, to find an ocean in a speech I wrote for people dressed in rags, but with really good asses.

I am "octal-coil-line-dancing," above ground, to carve my way along a narrow high, because in the mirror, I am gorging on red velvet cake, in my mask covered chin - number 30, carrying strawberries for breakfast. I think "they, numbers 100" should have a healthy fear of me- late at night, in the road, a healthy respect for any maniac or grim reaper passing along the coast. But for Arial, angel Ariel, this is important, that she may orgasm, that is very important to me, us, to us. That is very important to us.

To Sew The Night Together, At Last ~
Zachary Scott Hamilton

I get an internet connection and send this poem out in haste:

Drugs, New Orleans

_____
&&&&&&&&&&&&&&&&&&&&&&&&&&&&&&&&&&&&&&&&&&&&&
&&
^^

!!!!!!!!!!!!!!!!!!! (!
) !!!====
{&&&&&&&&&&&&&&&&&&&&&&&&&&}# # # # # # # # #
#
33333333333333333333333
((+)
....))
))****
****
_____
_____!!!!!!!!!!!!!!!!!!!!!!!!!!!!!!!!
!!!!!!!!!!!!!!!!!!!!!!!!!!!!!!++++++++++++++++++++++

$$
==

A curve of wife, cruel storm of shadows,
a thousand images they wet by in a
dream and take away your headache,
the storm crawls near on electric
alligator switchblade that the wife holds
dear to her black mass, a collapsing

shadow box there in her chest of oranges and rainbow antennae, as in a deeper thirst of rose thorns and barbed wire and electric lines, her power is but a massive growth she has learned to carry, and watching her eyes roll back while she is destroying with her trimming scissors neatly plucking at the dead leaves of those trees, to stray here is the wandering heart she cannot yet destroy in full, because tarp-shaped clowns wander up St. Claude watching the hours at great clocks made of tin foil and shoelaces, sheep skin and barnacles. A curve of the wrist, creole tongues lapping at the great water, tinsel, fish, pearl medallion drooling America, and neon, and blue hair from their stomachs, their shrimp guts,
their intestine, baked in flour, flopped and grilled, and fried and powdered. A yellow righteousness, crazed, insistent on gravy, and winning cheap shots of neon, and America, and blue hair. spin wheels rotating fabric space, thin circles round and round big white swooping throwing wheels, rotating, revolving and the place spins passed, hair all a retard.

Curling snack, snack, snack, snack,
curling rendezvous, and
let it be known the   turns, trigger fine hairs, speak a language under umbrella laughter, curling back a cloud or hay, a chimney or a mule, for a fourth night in paradise.

I havent gotten a response back. So I continue.

Shape the name in a small glare of legs in statues through window blinds

Legs of a runaway circuit raising a small confusion that marks purple lines in the rocks of the shore -- for a history. The fan blades another kind of parade already on the way as a centipede of laughter through a hundred legged puddles landing horizontal in their gloves --

After cars collide, two nights with a coy fish spinning in my gloves, along the wrist of the afternoon, I am dealt a hand of sun light and am drinking the moon --

And all of their ugly mirrors angled with the fishes, a language of wires, a tucking\

and intersecting of birds, a welded line of futures at the dripping-cloth-tongue all guessing and flannel and wooden --
Spiral down electric neckties, electric eye glasses -- To sew the night together at last

A beautiful, normal space and corner in time as well as the persona standing perched

at your front door -- you've made your mask and you smile inside this cloud and swim an eel infested distance.

Butterflies to down syrup ~ elongated in halogram -- blinking blue, red, neon feathers to stray --

-- TWO FISH --
To sew the night together, we need a rewinding hat, with an operating rodent on board, to get inside of the machine -- We will need (among other hanging

objects) a heating device, in which long strands of egyptian time may be pulled, thumb piano players all around the curtain room are playing Mozart, Bach, and Chopin -- Zeppelin, AC/DC, and Megadeath -- their masks blur at the edges of the room -- glowing ribs, and skulls, and spines -- We may need (among other, hanging objects) two double long bicycles, stacked with working (and yet glued together) radios, with antennae.

The sea will be our music (in at once,) splashing so forth, a mist of shanties along the glass bottle, and a ship for us inside -- hinges -- and door frames, wall paper, and galoshes for everyone aboard -- those who entertain the idea will be offered great woolen blankets, and a new pair of garments: shoes, and socks, powdered, first. Included are the radio bicycles (among other hanging things) which will spin the tale of the fish, and the water bearer -- the love entangled web of their story, to the sea together --
A dress -- a rabbit -- masks-- a russian hat -- ties -- wool shirts -- necklaces -- and

a harp -- Orchids -- sprays -- acrylic paints -- blankets -- bracelets, and jackets, and shoes! All will march in a parade of misguided watches!

To sew the night together, we will need to gather a bit of chalk for an over all out line of the moons slight, and subdued cubes, those sugars that drop, and dissolve near my boat in the lakeside -- by watching the curve of the swamp, and move of the frog, we will sew the night together at last --
Galoshes, and Russian hats for this night --
naked, amidst the neon making legs and arms and

handles of napes and necks out of knees and with neon tube, the whole lot of the night floating boating, and glowing every surface lined in color. Green to be blue, and sewing with Sewing Bee Orchestra on the barge, buried behind us, lovemaking neon lights -- all sewing together the edges, and fabrics, and colors of the night at last --

In the beginning of the shape -- of an elongation -- a fleur de lis, a lock of hair spinning --
trying to make clouds out of trumpeting horns and shattering drums --

Terms:

_____

THE SEA: A deep consciousness, closely related to that of companionship, a feeling that overwhelms the lovers. friendship.

HANDLES: "moustache with particularly lengthy and upwardly curved extremities; a shorter version is named the petit handlebar."

HARP: "a multi-string musical instrument which has the plane of its strings positioned perpendicularly to the soundboard."

TO SEW: to insist, and create a change that is irreversibly beautiful, and perfect in every measurable way for human and all other existing animal, mammal, fish, frog. Cow, Snake, Rat.

Notes: Dream Journal Excerpt (no. 1)

_____

A dark black cobblestone french quarter, where I was able to sneak back into my hovel, and wake early to the streets, with police passed out at bottles of Vodka, and beer, snoring while cats hopped passed and shuffled. Strangers lurked -- where I could even meet Brandy [Meesh ' ka] at a dark courtyard around the cobblestone street, near shops that opened up and a mechanical shapeshifting color animal rode on tracks, [around the dark abodes, on cobblestone pathways chasing cats and a girl all pale made me feel safe at the inside of an old,] french museum -- I could even sneak into hovels there with the furniture of victorians, all welded by hand. In the shadows of the ornate dream town -- This place was not a place for fears but for us

who could cross into the night. A **london maze** where spirits could hide in houses no longer forced to commiserate in the cobble streets. _____
The pale girl was happy to tell of all her most secret of sculptures and artistry's, as well as her best hiding places for us other creatures --

Waking to the sound of bulldogs, we notice a cat entering the squat on Rampart. Brandy says God sometimes uses animals to wake us up, and I say no its the cat they're barking at.

"This is a cat squat." I think.

[The wallpaper, peeled everywhere (must have been caught in hurricane Katrina.) Old boxes of tools, [can] see to the second floor through slats - paint chipping like old roman paintings - light comes in through white sheets molded over the doors, broken windows. Cat piss smell and old chairs stacked by ghosts, and holes in the floor everywhere, leading to a room in the other shotgun. A stack of encyclopedias is the most exciting thing i've seen in a long time... What used to be a fire place.]
The white cat sneaks to this area (...) ceiling caved in, at the back house, knocked out walls we enter through --
Brandy and I wrap in jackets, and sweaters for warmth, hold each other tight, breathing on each other for an organic heater.

We sing a song in our heads, while roaming the streets until we separate.
Drunk on gin, I yell: "Poem for a quarter!" on lundigras.
"Let us hear it." A man and his wife say.

Esplanade Clouds

Oh, how do we tie our hair
in the doll house windows, to the
cat, a length
all philadelphia telephone wires
as branches, our
cedar ties the hair back
in a willow rosetta, ornate
forget me nots, around bristle

spirals, winding one hand
through our hair even in
the sea at the epicenter,
french iron work, weaving
with algae, the eye of the
storm, a hurricane of celtic
cats, ornate
cats through
our hair - tied back into
pigtails in one
long pony tail to the sea,
and the moon --

| noon Aa. | ~ Zachary Scott Hamilton

On bundled fuchsia, the big, pink, and purple ligaments of straw ink, all German green, Gorging the dripping seeds spilled on the silverware; her hands painted white to the finger nails. Of fluids A rainbow, slower, of white doors, falling into the ocean, spiritual fingertips down her white arms, holding up the great American Idol. She holds a wad of 100 dollar bills, all together in a strip of tape, and lights the stove with gasoline. Gorging on the fuchsia, she cries, staring at the peach colored thread of the loveseat, and paints her self all of the way white, thrashing in panic, paranoid, seizures, and throws the perfectly wrapped hundreds in the large flames, her hands shaking; crumpled to a bowl of flowers, she rubs red paint onto her hands, washing in the flowers, and puts on a daily outfit of brown, chestnut tattered rags. She does her best to make her hair nice, but the red paint makes it difficult, and dirties her more. She wanders outdoors, begs men for money, her hands shake a tan hat with a few coins in it. A number of white trash scuba divers float in the back yard, in a few ft. of water, little neighbors rollerskate by, giving each other a ride on the refrigerator, and on the phone, with a little gurney they pull alongside full of telephones. The roosters peck on the tape recorder.

| noon Bb. |

Neighbor girls in white and cream throw a boy in the pool, screaming at least once for icecream, and kicking a scuba diver, until a gift is issued, tiny geniuses, girl subacute, scuba telephones, are finally starting to generate. Six clocks are brought to a tool shed, behind the house (three black, two white, and one red.) The moving company leaves the white clocks stacked on top of the black ones, on top of the red ones, and the shed doors are left open, so when she gets home, she can see the many different time zones. She has made seven dollars. In China this is pretty good, in Brazil she did okay, even in Alaska not bad, but by the time in New Orleans, she didn't make enough. Neighbors rollerskate by, and freeze, stop, roll straight, bend, contort, back and forth gliding to the card table in her lawn. Computerized by their own way of moving, like glass shards, blocks, and interference, the neighbors forming more than one picture of themselves, a six car pile up in the background, makes her neighbors rolling glitch movies as normal.

Especially The Ventures song that plays, and the blonde hair, a boy in a wrestling mask lights a firecracker, between mirrors, glass shard like chunks of a computer glitch, gliding the neighborhood, that generates around him explode slow.

| noon Cc. |

We're driving far. She gets into the blue Chevy nova 1977, and the engine starts up slow, and rumbling. Her makeup is done very well. It is not the same white you usually have on. He says, pulling out under the willow tree, the limbs scratching on the hood. He notices her eyeliner goes from bottom eyelid, to ear. She has touched up the upper eyelids with rainbow glitters, the lipstick is faint rum, her jet black haircut is recent, and long strings of it curl behind her rosy ear. She laughs, and pulls up her purse, warming up to the car, and pulls out cigarettes, and then straightens her jacket. He's been doing this staring contest with the lines in the road but speaks for a while about teaching coastal tradition, and she agrees with the few things he says.

George is your name, right? She winks, and he pulls the Chevy around behind a park, so the question can sink in. He checks his hair in the mirror after he parks. She rolls down the window and puffs at the cigarette. I'm moving away, Zoe. Wednesday night. The company has been curious about what my research paper entails, they want to bring me in for study. She is silent, and pulls smoke into her lungs. Lets it slowly down to her tongue.

[noon Dd.]

She walks in back, to the pool, and stands naked with blood red dress in her hands. The green swimming pool ripples her reflection, marbled face, and pale shoulders. She dresses, and jumps into the water, the red cloth slowing down around her, bubbling beneath her breasts- the banging in the nearby manican factory rumbles low, as she watches the dress float up to the surface, the blurred fabric, detaching slow from her skin; the information of early computers loads up and coarse through the water, squid memories chew into the computer code, slow men walk along with buffoon haircuts, they look at her body, memories of octopus, and rumba drums of the manicans drifted down into line, on the belt, the octopus entangles pieces of her dress, and for a moment, she cannot fight much, the octopus fades back to the soft red fabric, at the surface of the pool.

A dripping, alkaline dream, a wire of lace, organics, literally hair on broccoli, strand air, song, hills, leaning swerve, alkaline kiss, tops of the banyan trees, an eagle being wires, bent straw hat, permanent see through, waver frequency back up into the sky -

There were knots in the way that the ocean tied a part of the clouds, sunburned lining to crustaceans, the night is walking into the rain, the drawings drift

111

passed in our window, panthers we are smiling, and longing for them, they longing for panthers, and grip, just enough focus to continue playing our roles as children in the sky.

ZACHARY SCOTT HAMILTON lives in limbo, on the road, exploring art as life. He runs the small press Manican Haus, and can be found at infii2.weebly.com

Crown ~ Chris Holdaway

        The octopus is folding its granite body into foam. The internet misquotes scientists saying they're the best evidence we have for alien life on Earth, as though built in the prehensile mire is all the power of the Gulf Stream; to warp our view of the world.

      To say nothing of mushrooms that periscope in fields as surface-to-air missiles of extraterrestrial design. Fossils of androids wearing masks of dissected moon; skeins of bloodful flowers still holding somehow (leathery) in a gale;—

        though suppose I've never known a form of life that doesn't vomit its mycelium or infrastructure like the dew of flesh become weather.

      Gutters disappear under the canopy-cum-parasol of wood & plaster; wallpaper choking ceiling of vapours . . . There are shadows other than shadows, and the impotent clock cannot break anything, not with wax in my lungs (even arteries) as I drown in candles. The tile's sleep like dormant volcanic fields.

      You have the mouth of a river parasite or road marks lovelorn. There are joints in skin & sky. Our minds dispersed in the lost webbing between fingers, in a world where blood no longer leads the way.

—*after Aase Berg*

Silver Nitrate ~ Chris Holdaway

The bridge of my nose blooms into the sails of
    tallships sailing
From my skull; a person walking becomes
Fog in the diorama of taxidermied particles hung like
    a cloud.

Dawn is alongside everything. A terrifyingly resolute cork
Filling space; clothed in radiation. I've been so much
    this day

. . .

Buried beneath a mirror; an hourglass mound of
    powdered
        Glass; a pyre of increased surface area

                —if anyone is there is anyone left?

                                —*after Alejandra Pizarnik*

A Wax Museum ~ Chris Holdaway

Numerology is any belief in events yet for more than one moment it has been raining between you & the wall; you & the elephantine heart looming deadcentre of the room—you & the nearby star. You try to grasp its recalcitrant architecture but slip incessant because is it convex or concave encircled(?)—try to orbit joyous like swinging from a lamppost singing with the old sun, explosive clouds, or red mountain in the crook of your elbow.

(there is no evidence for analysis; as if there would be precise dimensions to famine to elaborate demonstrations of death . . . The number of fish making an allusion to fish scaling into every one of your trillion trilobite cells)

Time to fall like a chained prisoner asleep against the fused chambers, a sleep that claws open eyes as if the air were too thick for your lashes, letting nothing but the heartsun's burning tick through.—it takes only a drop of blood to turn a whole glass of water red. You unfold the bulk of wet velvet beating in split time, flatten it like longwinded wallpaper with three repeating flowerheads; five tessellating smokestacks; eight dripping grilles in a stormwater drain. A veneer of numbers but above all the smell of pastelcoloured shampoo bottles, ash, & ferrous black sand in the soup . . . Look(!) light is crushing itself like blinded sparrows against a window without sides, leaving frozen lace to track with fingernails in the glass. Spot three woollen moths weighed down by their tasteless bodies, & four dozen wet fallen leaves or slugs engorged on rust &/or blood.

This is your adult form, wondering how the solar tissue you stretched like unprimed canvas still ticks from inside nowhere. So tired as you feel waves of empire you recite dramatic figures like the fading areas of icecaps, the wandering aridity line, the sealevel rises to drown out the clock as if it were lungs, not a heart. It's hard to find the pound of flesh lost with all the weight you're gaining through the depthless cut teeth of this keyhole birth. The air is being marched from its lands and soon will be so tightly packed nothing will be able to move for breath. Everyone sinks to the ground for more than one moment, then floats up to bob on the surface of the atmosphere—draped like gilt linen of the finest threadcount.

—*after Unica Zürn*

Turing Test: Tree ~ Chris Holdaway

TWO ROOMS WITH SOME ARRANGEMENT FOR COMMUNICATING

A tree sits at your table of broadleaf, coniferous, evergreen

Death—a figure consistent with random guessing.

Is it possible a tree is a calendar, a chemical

Added hand taking a syringe to the air or itself just a spike

Of atmosphere? Turtle on its back in the standard

Interpretation—in virtual north, virtual tropics, virtual

rainforest—, the interrogator limited by the grain

Of bark & tree rings running perpendicular.

A computer is identified by speed that has nothing

To do with its body image rendering

Autopsies of pine, fig, or otherwise beyond us. Thin leaves

Have no power of redaction over so many

Versions of the wrong decision.

;—Can there be dew without grass?
  I'm a gilded swamp.

;—What is a 30-story building?
  A garden of locusts.

;—Where are your friends?
  I traded my bark for whaleskin.

;—Would you go to war?
  Few can eat needles.

;—A warhead has no tree rings.
  But the ash explains.

;—Are you trying to impress me?
  Explosions refuse to stay local.

;—You can radiocarbon date a person too.
  Knight's armour turned diving bell.

Ghost Column ~ Chris Holdaway

The sky lowers the sea into place; clouds leaden with
silver, & a star between the forks of a crescent moon.
Birds shriek in the cage of a small
Room muffled by the ends of the earth, by physics of
library stacks & desklamps that could bloom into
mushroom clouds. If dust is dead skin I mean to ask
how   dense   with   corpse   is   the   air?
A glacier develops like photograph paper, melts
precisely into a chessboard with no pieces. There is no
way away, the museum matte painting behind
everything through some trick of depth heatmoulded
to the surface of my eyes . . . Dropped from a great
height I
pierce the zeppelin skin
Of earth choked full of gas, fallen into a fault line that
becomes a ribcage—peeling my own skin
until all slotted bones resemble stormwater drains.
O,
The consequences of a halfsmile—trepanned by
particularly strong rain drops. Clothes beyond
smelling of dirt, clutching a severed forearm spouting
blood like a bottle of champagne I can't afford. A
bundle of neutrons arranged like flowers; I wear a
baroque ruff as a neckbrace, a raincloud suspended in
a wheelchair. Hinges rust, become metamorphic then
twentyfour bits of information.
My postal address no longer works because
Of rising sea levels & continental drift.

"Camerman Of The Soil" ~ Chris Holdaway

Every visit just makes me want to write about bones
Becoming storms, and bricks shrink until the house
   falls around
Its loose mortar. Oh, just like my shoelaces. Pull
A thread of nervous system from my ear and sew
Chain links back in . . .
              I opened my arm, skin parted fibrous like
The muscle tissue that should be under-
neath. I poured in sap as a kind
Of reverse tree torture. Insects were there, itching
At my media, shifting asymptotically
More than their body weights. (Somehow
In a forest of people looking up.) My favourite past
Time is observing constellations from latitudes where
That isn't possible; as if I could make the sun rise and set
A new record. Someone's water breaks onto silver
Platters, and I've eaten so
Many hollow grapeskins my stomach has filled
In with the flesh. Even the thinnest piece of paper or
   tenderest leather
Has an anatomy,—I would have no problems
Making them from humans at all.

CHRIS HOLDAWAY *is a poet / editor / linguist from New Zealand. He directs Compound Press, & is a candidate in the MFA programme at Notre Dame. He received his MA(Hons) in linguistics from the University of Auckland, where he also studied cosmology & astrophysics.*

A Dream Of Blue Sunlight ~ Douglas Thompson

Whisper wind-swept forests in my ear, the memory of your blood red lips. You left the living room a few lifetimes ago, an ocean crossed the ceiling, clocks turning upside down. Your narcotic voice still echoes my head as the plexiglass baby commences its inexplicable crawl across the polished floorboards, creepy-crawly movements, jerky, twitchy. Like a drop of molten glass, quartz, liquid sunlight, what the hell? You said you were leaving it in my safe-keeping, putting on your fur coat and scarf, making an exit. And now the keys in the door are rattling, Pauline returning home. What am I to do or make of this? I have a vague feeling of guilt, like maybe you and I made the plexiglass baby together. Keeping one eye on it, half-turning my head, I sense the danger it might crawl under some furniture. This disturbs me some. Guilt and worry, none of it for anything sane or normal.

All the rules are failing, drifting, gravity no longer holds in the corridors of the city of Spindrift. Ours is no exception. I screwed on the handrails last autumn, at the recommended random angles to ceilings and walls. I float between them like an astronaut as I make my way to greet Pauline coming in the door. She opens her mouth and all the words roll out low and slow, upside down, one of several altered principles. I talk too, concealing my vague guilt with a torrent of humdrum irrelevance wrapped in conversational orange peel and rose petals.

Back in the living room we touch down again into normal physics. I can still remember your voluptuous feline smell, is it still all over me? Will Pauline notice? And Christ, where's the plexiglass baby? Just like I feared, trying to let my eyes scan the room casually, without giving away my desperation and fear too much: it's escaped into some nook or cranny or cubby-hole, as tiny transparent babies do. Wait. Do they? How would I or anyone know? This is nuts of course, but unquestionable as ever, we must simply press ahead with life, all pretend we know the rules which no one has ever read and have never been written down anywhere anyway. Let Heisenberg write a formula for it.

A whale is beached on our lawn, dining on a dessert of fine crystal chandeliers stolen from City Hall on the last tsunami he must have caught a ride through like a night bus for sleepy drunks. He seems happy enough, but the local children will tether him down if we don't stop them and doom him soon to be a bouncy castle. The green grass out there is screaming in the yellowing afternoon light. Yellow of old tusks and custard tarts. But now as I prepare Pauline's dinner whilst wearing my sharkskin apron I catch sight of the baby again, out of the corner of my eye, climbing up the corner of the dining room like a transparent tarantula. Can Pauline even see it? She follows my gaze suspiciously but seems unperturbed. I'm too scared to ask her. Instead I wait until the next time she goes to the toilet and lunge for it, catching the baby in my right hand, feeling it struggling, stuffing it in my pocket before she gets back. It writhes, feels rubbery but super-indestructible, babe on a mission, like some kind of up-scaled sperm, trying to find the ovules of our house, to impregnate our boiler cupboard or our electricity meter or some other weird shit.

The phone rings, or the whole wall does rather, the usual pattern of pulsating lights, translated into words by the City Fathers' historical transposition gizmo. *It's your brother Dorrance...* Pauline smiles warmly, brushing her hair back into a clasp. *I love his voice. Where's the popcorn?*

That's odd. The plexiglass baby seems to have just stopped wriggling, as if it is in some way connected to my brother. Now how can that be?

Tell me again, Pauline sighs, reclining back into an armchair, *just how you can have a brother a thousand years old.*

I've explained it before, I mutter, *my mother won a New Scientist competition and got the chance to have one of her embryos frozen, meaning me. Dorrance got born and grew up in a world destined to drown itself. I got born here and grew up to meet you, you lucky girl you.*

And how can he talk to us? –Pauline yawns.

Spindriftian ingenuity is all. Time-tunnelling. The City Fathers open random time windows in the walls of the apartments of numerous people in the drowned past. They got lucky one day and found my brother, thought I might like to talk to him and update them occasionally on anything useful I learn about our past.

Greetings, sibling. Today in Edinburgh, I caught a tram past the Scott Monument. Imagine that, a hundred-foot high Victorian stone monument to a writer, Sir Walter Scott, inspired by a ruined abbey in one of his novels. Imagine a world where writers could be so revered. Today's equivalent would have to be a footballer or a celebrity plumber. Or a chef of course. A hundred foot high sculpture of one of Jamie Oliver's fucking cheese soufflés. It's been raining now for forty-three days in a row. Is this the start of that forthcoming great inundation you told me about? Will I ever see the sunlight again in my own lifetime? Should I build a boat on top of Ben Nevis?

Pauline nudges me, nods at the screen.

Wait, wait, Bro! Pauline wants to know what a tram is.

*

I wake up in the middle of the night, gagging, trying to cry out, scream, with the plexiglass baby at my throat, its sharp mik-teeth digging into my throat, its chubby little fingers trying to gouge my eyes out. Somehow I get it loose and hurl it across the room. It hits the wall with a satisfying smack and slides down leaving a slithery silvery trail on the wall, picked out in the moonlight from our slightly-parted curtains. I am shocked for a moment at what I have done. But it was self-defence. Amazingly, Pauline turns over sleepily, not having heard my struggles, presuming it to be one of my attacks of nocturnal stomach acid. Furious, revolted, I steel myself, pick the foul little demon up and rush through to the kitchen and throw it in the sink, pour cold water on it, racking my brains, trying to buy time to think what to do.

I finally decide to put it into the microwave for three minutes. When the door springs open, there is no odour, only a little black figure climbing down eventually, shell-shocked, staggering, weaving like a drunk, leaving dark toe-prints across the kitchen floor as it makes his way towards the living room windows. To my astonishment, the footprints slowly disappear behind it and its own black form gradually regenerates back to transparent again, a few black ashes fallen off blowing hither and thither across the lounge then disintegrating into infinitesimal dust. It is indestructible, not of this world. It isn't even angry, remains silent as ever. It seems to have its own mission, whatever it is, to which I am incidental. Then why try to strangle me? As if hearing these thoughts, it turns around now, from where it's been standing at the window, gazing out calmly into the landscapes of suburban night. I'd swear its little dark eyes are watching me. What the hell does it want?

*

On the drive in to the city centre I pass the eastern business district, and have to pause with the other drivers to let it all shuffle past us. Timber buildings constructed on posts and wheels, the City Fathers have decreed that one of its periodic repositionings must happen, presumably to avoid the latest flood lines and squall pockets. All the streets in Spindrift are rotated and shifted at least once a month throughout the year. The taxi drivers are Einsteins.

*

City Hall is a vast circular structure made from the inward curving beams of whale ribs. Red and pink light spills from the glazed fissures in its bone outer structure, seemingly discolouring the bleak grey afternoon cloudscape behind it. Constant spattering of raindrops, our city-island is aptly-named. Spindrift, sea spray, spume. Inside I find Councillor Mountebank climbing out of his giant automated crab shell, a two-seater. His secretary drives it away, the orange carapace hinging back down. An afternoon's debating in parliament consists of fifty crabshells jousting and smashing each other up like this. He looks remarkably unrattled.

We turn into a corridor together and briefly lose our gravity. He points out the appropriate handles to me and I traverse the ceiling like a cliff face, catching up with him, shouting after him as we go. *Just why does this keep happening, councillor? I don't remember it so bad when I was a kid.*

Time-tunneling, my good man, it takes its toll. Fuck with gravity and gravity fucks with you. Once we've finally finished re-writing history we can hopefully put it all back together again and sew up the unravelled sleeve of care. Some of us will need multiple stitches though, eh? I smile woodenly, but he always loses me.

In one of his consulting rooms, vaulted chamber of chequered marble tiles, I unfold my hold-all and lay out a shoe box on the table, bound tightly closed with gaffer tape but with air holes just in case. When I get the lid off, I watch his eyes carefully. Can he see the thing? He turns his head sideways, narrows his eyes, reaches for some special red goggles from a shelf behind him.

What are those? I ask, as I reach out and push the baby back in the box as it begins writhing, waking up. *X-ray, Infra-red? Can you see this, councillor, or am I losing my mind? Is it old world technology? Twentieth century? Twenty-first?*

Much older than that, I fear... he almost whispers. *Medieval. Fascinating... Have you heard of alchemy? Cold fusion? Necromancy? Homunculi... Latin for little man. Artificial life contrived directly from the seed. He's still seeking out the ova, the great egg of life, the transparent world globe upon which we tentatively tip-toe with bare feet, weather sloshing around below like chemical elements, clouds of silver-nitrate. Like an hour-glass, we keep tipping it upside down.*

Councillor, I'm afraid I haven't the slightest idea what you're talking about... I reach out and nudge his arm, as if waking him up.

What? He looks around startled, takes his red goggles off. *No, quite. Me neither. You're clearly suffering from paranoid delusions. We both are. You need to go get some rest. For my part, I think I need to go get drunk and write my will. Last time this happened it presaged the end of the world. But cheer up, son, no man is an island...* He squints at me, smiling weakly. *As for the little guy, well. If I were you I'd concentrate really hard on the idea that you're in a dream and none of this is actually happening.*

*

I pause the car on the way back, take a different turning from usual, drive south along the west coast. The latest tsunami has shifted the shoreline again, whole villages gone underwater, the decades-old ruins of drowned ones brought back to the surface. I put on the brakes, can go no further, lean out of the window to admire an eerie spectacle that has fascinated me since childhood: the sight of tarmac streets and crossroads with painted white lines, all vanishing out under the water, leading away and down, as if off into dreams and sleep, lost linking pathways to an inverted world, where the past still lives on, love can be endlessly rekindled, water can be breathed.

I get out and walk through the blackened ruins of what was once someone's living room, perhaps only ten years ago. I marvel at the dishonoured tokens of suburban individualism, of once-happy family life. The framed pictures on the walls, painted scenes now just blotches of seaweed and sphagnum, sofa swollen like a voracious sponge. The bathtub has fish swimming in it. The ex marital bed is a coral reef.

I hear a noise behind me and make my way back out onto what was once a street. The plexiglass baby is tapping on the car window, for all the world like an abandoned dog, demanding to be taken walkies. I get in and drive to the nearest beach, but it refuses to get out there, climbs over into the back seat and picks up the road atlas in its teeth and brings it forward to me, spreads it open across my lap and thumps its little fist at one particular bay, not far from your house. Makes its first ever vocalisation: an unpleasant little grunt, more animal than human. We can be there in fifteen minutes.

*

At the bay, a crazy old fisherman greets us, his eyes looking in two different directions at once, neither of them focused on any recognisable reality. Tells me he saw a woman meeting your description here two days ago, before the big wave. Says you were walking a small dog, but it got into difficulty in the rock pools far out as the tide was coming in. He'd shouted to her not to risk herself, had phoned the coastguard. Then the crunch came. White-out, this whole side of the island.

I look down at the baby and wonder if the fisherman can see it, turn to check his gaze then realise the pointlessness. Wish I'd followed the dog analogy through and improvised some kind of leash for the little bastard. It seems eager to get going, but it's as if it's been listening, absorbing all this information like I have. Or rather, as if it knows it all already, is just eager to watch me observe and digest.

The plexiglass baby makes its way jerkily, over and among the rock-pools. With the cautious motion of a crab, the glistening transparency and consistency of a jellyfish. It's working its way down the rocky beach, as if seeking something out like a bloodhound... heading for the waves. Can it breathe underwater? –As all babies must pre-birth within the amniotic sac? I walk after it, both horror-stricken and enchanted, drawn on, divided deep within myself, between curiosity and revulsion. The waves are breaking, sea rolling and broiling, spraying spume. Soon it reaches the water, tastes the salt and cold, but scarcely hesitates, keeps on going. It advances relentlessly, will soon be gone where I cannot follow. I fall to my knees, dig my fingers deep into the miserable grey sand.

*

Next day, I wake up on the floor of the fisherman's ramshackle old beach hut, my bones cold and sore from an uncomfortable night, tormented by black dreams. I stand up and stagger out into the uncertain morning light, a pale blue sky and bitter fresh wind picking up from the north. The tide has gone out. I walk slowly, stiffly, with a feeling of premonition like a man condemned, down the long sands towards the retreating edge of the freezing sea.

Your black hair is tangled among the seaweed, almost indistinguishable at first. Your skin is white as fish flesh, your red dress stained dark as wilted roses.

I approach like a worshipper, kneel as a priest. Akin to a slow-moving snail, the baby has left a still-gleaming trail of slime across the rocks, has crawled up your smooth inside leg, penetrated beneath the rough folds of your ruined dress. I take your shoulders and turn you over, shaking and shivering all the time, feeling for a pulse in your cold, dead neck. Christ, your lovely face, the emotion heaves up from inside me, shakes me apart. I lay my head upon your chest and close my eyes, tears spilling from tightly closed lids, muttering and wailing incoherently.

A great empty space filled only by the swishing of the wind and hypnotic sighs of the waves. After an age, I feel cold, impossible fingers brush the back of my neck. I pull back, sit up, startled, saying your name. Just as I both dread and hope: your eyes flick open. But black as night, they are not your own.

~

DOUGLAS THOMPSON *was a director and chair of The Scottish Writers' Centre from 2011 to 2014. His short stories and poems have appeared in a wide range of magazines and anthologies. He won the Grolsch/Herald Question of Style Award in 1989 and second prize in the Neil Gunn Writing Competition in 2007. His first book, Ultrameta, was published by Eibonvale Press in August 2009, nominated for the Edge Hill Prize, and shortlisted for the BFS Best Newcomer Award, and since then he has published eight subsequent novels and short story collections: Sylvow (Eibonvale Press, 2010); Apoidea (The Exaggerated Press, 2011); Mechagnosis (Dog Horn Publishing, 2012); Entanglement (Elsewhen Press, 2012); The Rhymer (Elsewhen Press, 2014); The Brahan Seer (Acair Books, 2014); Volwys (Dog Horn Publishing, 2014); The Sleep Corporation (The Exaggerated Press, 2015).*

douglasthompson.wordpress.com/

∞ ~ Socrates Martinis

Two tangential circles are drawn around her feet forming the sign of infinity, a horizontal eight, an antique key bow, the crank of a mechanical toy or the lower part of a pubic bone. With her ankles tied to the shadow-less pillar of a sundial, Night walks stretching behind her two long chords. On this lyre inscribed in the field morning birds will sit as the fingers of Orpheus. While laying the eggs of dawn she looks at the horizon line through a pair of reversed opera binoculars.

∞ ~ Socrates Martinis

Δύο εφαπτόμενοι κύκλοι είναι γραμμένοι γύρω από τα πόδια της σχηματίζοντας το σημείο του απείρου, ένα οριζόντιο οκτώ, την κεφαλή ενός παλιού κλειδιού, τη μανιβέλα μηχανικού παιχνιδιού ή το κάτω μέρος του ηβικού οστού. Με τους αστραγάλους δεμένους στον χωρίς σκιά στύλο ενός ηλιακού ωρολογίου, η Νύχτα βαδίζει τεντώνοντας πίσω της δύο μακριές χορδές. Πάνω σε αυτή τη λύρα που εγγράφεται στο πεδίο, τα πουλιά του πρωινού θα καθίσουν όπως τα δάχτυλα του Ορφέα. Καθώς γεννάει τα αβγά της αυγής, κοιτάζει τον ορίζοντα μέσα από ένα ανάποδο ζευγάρι κιάλια της όπερας.

The sabotage of dawn ~ Socrates Martinis

From the clogs within the final rotation of nocturnal hours, smoke rose with the smell of roasted chicken. The moustached sphinx got off his bicycle and entered the grand hall of the railway station, where silence swelled like a puff of air in the ears of an emerging swimmer, carrying a basket of dead roosters. Our morning is a lamp behind a white sheet.

Η δολιοφθορά της αυγής ~ Socrates Martinis

Από τα γρανάζια εντός της τελικής περιστροφής των νυχτερινών ωρών, καπνός σηκώθηκε με τη μυρωδιά ψητού κοτόπουλου. Η (Ο) μυστακοφόρος σφίγξ κατέβηκε από το ποδήλατο και μπήκε στη μεγάλη αίθουσα του σιδηροδρομικού σταθμού, όπου η σιωπή φούσκωνε όπως μια πνοή του αέρα στα αυτιά αναδυόμενου κολυμβητή, κρατώντας ένα καλάθι με νεκρούς πετεινούς. Το πρωί μας είναι μια λάμπα πίσω από λευκό σεντόνι.

132

The Flowering Wall ~ Socrates Martinis

As she hangs
a fish from the belfry
the love-struck geometer
draws
on his window
the angles
of her armpit
and
straight lines
connecting
the beauty mark
on her moving forearm

Το ανθισμένο τείχος ~ Socrates Martinis

Καθώς εκείνη κρεμάει
ένα ψάρι απ' το καμπαναριό
ο ερωτοχτυπημένος γεωμέτρης
γράφει
στο παράθυρό του
τις γωνίες
της μασχάλης της
και
ευθείες γραμμές
που ενώνουν
την ελιά
στον κινούμενό της βραχίονα

Morning Horse ~ Socrates Martinis

In the morning
the angular
echo
of the East
is engraved
on
the statue
of a horse head
indicated
by the
five-fingered shadow
of her left hand
on the wall

Άλογο του πρωινού ~ Socrates Martinis

Το πρωί
η γωνιώδης
ηχώ
της Ανατολής
χαράσσεται
πάνω στο
άγαλμα
ενός κεφαλιού αλόγου
που υποδεικνύεται
από την
πενταδάκτυλη σκιά
του αριστερού χεριού της
στον τοίχο

Egg ~ Socrates Martinis

Scissors cut
the bride's equator
tied as a coil
An egg slides
between her feet
A shining egg
A cannon ball
A blue sphere
A nut shell
A star

Αυγό ~ Socrates Martinis

Κόπηκε με ψαλίδι
ο ισημερινός της νύφης
μπλεγμένος σαν πηνίο
Ένα αυγό κυλάει
ανάμεσα στα πόδια της
Ένα αυγό λαμπερό
Μια μπάλα κανονιού
Μια μπλε σφαίρα
Ένα καρυδότσουφλο
Ένα αστέρι

SOCRATES MARTINIS was born in Athens, Greece in 1984. He has published two books of poetry and ink sketches (both in Greek and English) on Editions Farfoulas ("Small Hand of Bronze", 2010) and More Mars Team ("North", 2014). He has appeared on "Sein und Werden" and "The Fractured Nuance" magazines. He has also published several works of experimental/ electroacoustic music on various international labels like Absurd, Drone records, Entr'acte, Antifrost etc.

Jellyfish, 1-7 ~ Owen Vince

*

*fluorescent you – is aching with
red, orange, golden -
withdrawing.*

*

*thousand you - replacing
empty water, with translucence
- skin.*

*

*barbarous you - something
with quality
of light, width of motion. Calmly.*

*

*poisonous you – sugaring the
undertow, knowing -
nothing.*

*

*somnolent you - sour
cupped mind,
this love. This -*

*

*graciously you - the reversal
of light ; on, and then
off.*

*

*shimmering you - being
beyond being, & blossom
carefully. Aniseed, i recall*

Six Fallen Towers ~ Owen Vince

I.
lovely girl, she - falling hair bunched up - is
look! You have four fingers and a thumb! I am in
love with this, its arcade music.

II.
the architecture is understood like map and, at night,
as distant light -
everybody has left the room, abandoning shoes,
leaving scarves hooked over railings.

III.
treatment mouth, in a sense of -
not wanting to be here. The tight roundabout before
clinic. Its sudden white walls.

IV.
self-murder, as in; the fucked completing of a circle -
my gold or yellow seeming bedroom clothes. I
remember being there, in a room, with you -

V.
thinking, there must be something else -
beyond this dismal shining life. Where to begin.
Patient little steps – to - cavernous thing.

VI.
the river in Cambridge in winter blue -
the thin branched arms of the trees. A coral lip.
Panting.

What Did We Do To Deserve Dogs In Automatic
~ Owen Vince

dog swallowing rainbow has half-completed the
  mesmeric
de-attachment described in books that are good for
  its now
unwavering with teeth to sugar the very thin partition
between "this" and - i guess - "that" complex
mysterious
place its tumble of unbelted wavering columns its
  pitchfork
skies -

darling i have no great love for rain it can agitate the
  skin or
drown cities and make living in them unbearable ;
  saw you hold
your fingertips in basket shape as if to collect falling
  substance
the shimmering dropped rainbow ; i remember being
  shocked
how attuned you were to the colour of outer space
  its morbid
antique bossanova playing to a harpsichord with dog
leaping unsheltered into the vast girdled rainbow
  moon - i heard its bark
dislodge the world , saw its prints like big upside-
  down faces walk
across the skin of orion leaving marks | its very
  unusual bilbao orange.

The Watchers, Alton Estate ~ Owen Vince

[one]
to displace marble – you say it
participates first
through blackness | across
hillside, to estate's
mass its colourlessness, and has no oversight
of them – as if to say
"look!" - and fail
to see what is reported missing,
what is pushing grapes into its mouth
in hospital wards.
Of course,
I cherish nothing
these days. I also pray more.

[two]
Stand, patient in the
perched & beaten
fabric, and stable now.
Now
is at rest. Is, valiant.
Sees? Fluoride, embankment, it threatens you
with total policing, the knife fight.
Christmas tears.
Every second I regretted leaving.
And Wario is there.

[three]
Perched-legged body
with unknown face ; reads,
'I remain', like, mountainside
talk. Rubble, the underside
of buildings – it is echoing.

[four]
With air raid memories
old men are not dancing
and ask, 'is this culture?',
as rain slaps
against the bowed thin glass.

'I don't know'

the noise that cockpits make.
the noise that doors closing make.

[five]
often, 'fish like, sometimes
coloured', their beaten bronze,
beaten the air
through working you reach -
form, stance, balance,
line. The attitudes
of bent steel radiate
to frame,   as if it were
a building, and this

[six]
a preparation -
into volume, into unfixed
unaffected
space, giving the effect of mass, the vitality
of line – bleak, rough contour. Like, faces -
aggressive seeming at first,
and then calm,
and then – only, loving. The sighing black gold
mastiff bends its muzzle and shocks you
into babble saying rain
 is one part water. Rain
 is one part water.
 Rain is one part.

From "Sequenes For The Rothko Chapel" ~
Owen Vince

[t.ten]
horses, their terrible blindness | a type of
behaviour on rolling planes like | water and its
transaction between copper pipes and
deadliness or | a meat served usually hot in
bread is | the sound heard at night from the
mist-blanketed fields that are | animals noted
for their size beauty and speed | are also
known to be | carriers of plague at least as we
all are carriers of it.

[e.eleven]
parasite! The bowed crab headed soft address,
the pearl-coloured nightclubs with all so much
swinging in which I at last aged, stuttered |
spilling my drink over new shoes and hers,
gasping like a fish on aluminium beaches and
at last had the sense to scream into the blank
midnight air, I am lost || but that is,
eventually, a place for all of us ; all of us.

[t.twelve]
dominant forms of transport, like ; my hands
carrying rubbish and potato skins and
discarded bottles from the old house into the
street | where everything has begun changing
into winter colours, has new brittle lights and
saw-tooth edges || so as to appear less soft
and more brilliant, the colours that associate
with diamond, + do everything they can to
breathe.

Before The Rothko Chapel ~ Owen Vince

[a]
in the garden, she bends to adjust
a shoe - above her
the sky is
a glass tower, which
also bends. Everything
is both morning
and midnight; a brittle Texas
colour; sandpaper
in a glass of sugar water -
almost , immanence.

OWEN VINCE *is a poet, arts critic, and editor of PYRAMID Editions poetry press. His work has recently appeared or is upcoming in* Envoi, gobbet, Atrocity Exhibition, t.NY.Press, *and* Elbow Room. *He has a chapbook of poems due later this year with White Knuckle Press, and tweets @abrightfar*

**Summer Kissed Everyone Underwater ~
Katherine Osborne & Bob Schofield**

Never swim to
the lighthouse during a party

I collect friendships and send
microscopic love notes to your fish bowl

Did you find yourself
wanting human contact

Or could you dream in a beam of silk

**We Made Armies To Lift The Night Mattress ~
Katherine Osborne & Bob Schofield**

Blink for me
without showing your brilliant son

He floods the internet
with pictures

A snowy owl
unzips its cloud

& falls straight down his tree machine

Disappearing Forests Reveal Tall Strangers ~
Katherine Osborne & Bob Schofield

My mouth is a wilderness
that can't break up with you
over the intercom

I am sweeping glass lions
from the treehouse

You are kind to the kidnappers

They built you clouds
so that no one
will hear the screams

Is there something
tapping

      above the branches?

Most Spies Look Like Caged Trees ~
Katherine Osborne & Bob Schofield

You talk about capturing meteors in Spain

The last zoo can't respond if you
pretend to drown in quicksand

I found two plastic horses on my mountain

They will show us
landscapes with no malls

A complicated vessel
moves to erase our tracks

The Sky Has Two Bad Grades ~
Katherine Osborne & Bob Schofield

Call me through dark leaves

I press all the wrong digits
inside my dream
of mopeds beeping

Did God scream at you about oceans
or blood interstates? Masks that appear
when prehistoric beans become self-
aware computers that predict
the end of bees?

My town was abandoned

Then tourists nested inside the payphone
No one remembers the explosion in caves
No one remembers puddles No one
speaks anymore

Just you

*KATHERINE OSBORNE is a writer in Massachusetts
and editor of Little River.*

*BOB SCHOFIELD is the writer and illustrator of The
Inevitable June. He likes what words and pictures
do. He'd like to be a ghostly presence in your life.*